ICY HERITAGE

COVER:
Cape Evans, the base of the British Antarctic Expedition (1910-13).
Colin Monteath / Hedgehog House New Zealand.

ICY HERITAGE

The historic sites of the Ross Sea Region, Antarctica.

by *DAVID L. HARROWFIELD*

To George with very warm regards
Mawson's huts Cape Denison Antarctica
19 December 2008
David L. Harrowfield

ANTARCTIC HERITAGE TRUST : 1995

ISBN 0-473-03232-5

Published by:
Antarctic Heritage Trust
P.O. Box 14-091, Christchurch
New Zealand

With assistance from The Stout Trust

Designed and Printed for the Publisher by:
The Caxton Press, Christchurch, New Zealand

Contents

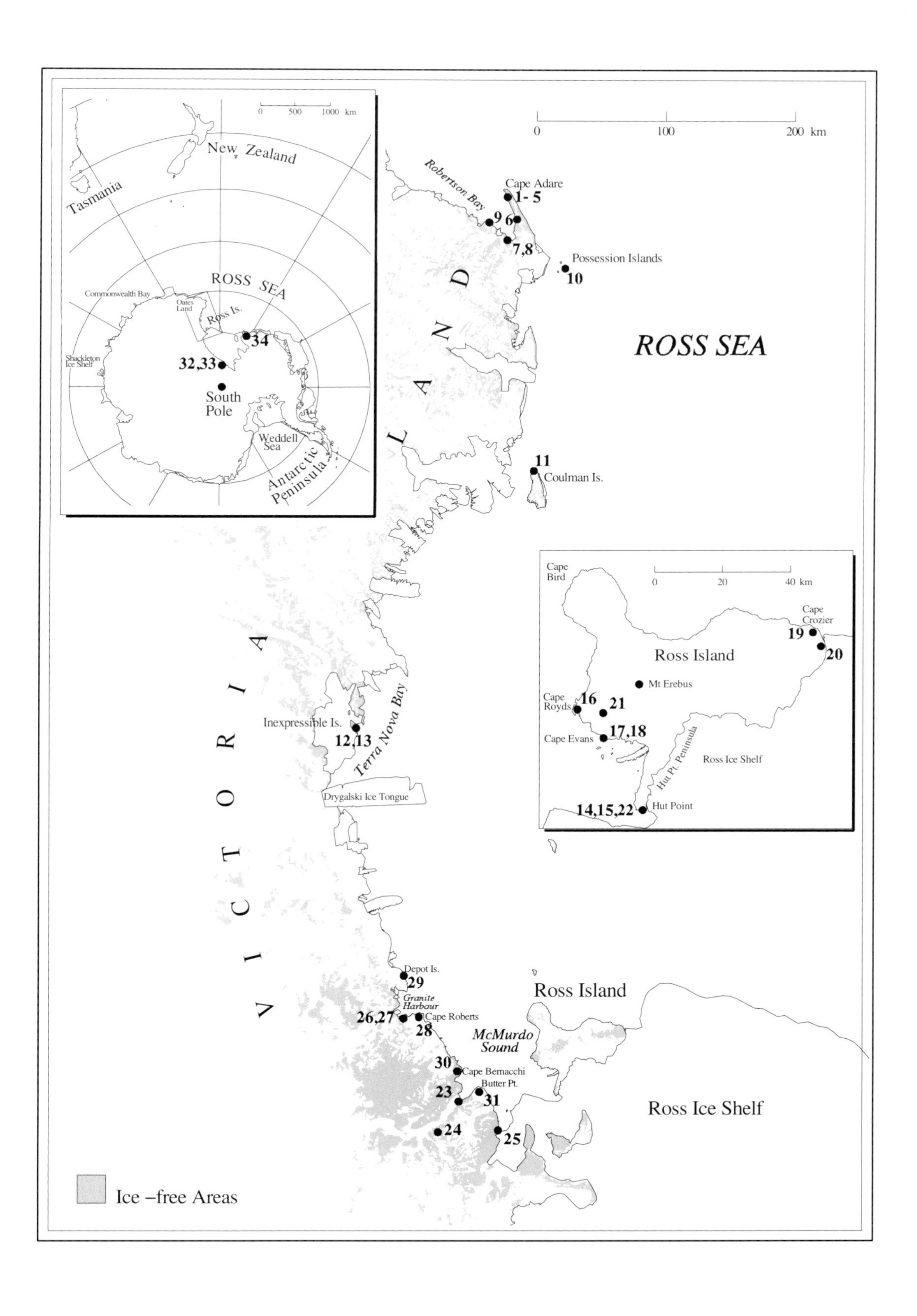

0 500 1000 km
New Zealand
Tasmania
ROSS SEA
Commonwealth Bay
Oates Land
Ross Is.
34
32,33
Shackleton Ice Shelf
South Pole
Weddell Sea
Antarctic Peninsula
0 100 200 km
Robertson Bay
Cape Adare
1- 5
9
6
7,8
Possession Islands
10
ROSS SEA
11
Coulman Is.
V I C T O R I A L A N D
Inexpressible Is.
12,13
Terra Nova Bay
Drygalski Ice Tongue
Cape Bird
0 20 40 km
Cape Crozier
19
20
Ross Island
Mt Erebus
Cape Royds
16
21
17,18
Cape Evans
Hut Pt. Peninsula
Ross Ice Shelf
14,15,22
Hut Point
Depot Is.
29
Granite Harbour
26,27
Cape Roberts
28
Ross Island
McMurdo Sound
30
Cape Bernacchi
Butter Pt.
23
31
24
25
Ross Ice Shelf
Ice –free Areas

DEDICATION

To Dr Trevor Hatherton
OBE, POLAR MEDAL, B.SC, DIC, PHD, DSC(HONS), FRSNZ
(1924-1992)

Chairman Ross Dependency Research Committee (1983-89)
President of the Royal Society of New Zealand (1985-89)
Founder and Patron, Antarctic Heritage Trust (1987-1992)

Dr Trevor Hatherton has done more than anyone else to put New Zealand's flag on the Antarctic map.

He was a leader and a pioneer in the early days when nations were still coming to grips with the notion of an international Antarctic community.

A world-class geophysicist and President of the Royal Society of New Zealand, he brought good science to the ice and earned the world's respect for New Zealand's place as a Treaty nation.

He leaves behind one of his finest contributions—the Antarctic Heritage Trust —largely his own personal mission—to oversee and manage the preservation of historic sites on the ice. In his footsteps follows a well-organised group dedicated to this cause.

This important heritage is further secured, thanks to the legacy and leadership of Trevor Hatherton.

Bob Norman Q.S.O., B.E.(HONS),
M.SC.(HONS), F.I.P.E.N.Z.
Associate Patron, Antarctic Heritage Trust.

Dr Trevor Hatherton outside Shackleton's hut, Cape Royds.NZAP (Chris Rudge)

Foreword

It's hard to believe that the 'heroic-era' of Antarctic exploration only took place around the first decade of the 20th century. Names such as Scott, Amundsen, Shackleton and Mawson epitomise adventure in British, and indeed world history.

For those of us who travelled the Antarctic continent in the early days of vehicles, aircraft and radio communications, it is hard to grasp how lonely it must have been for the first explorers who had no contact with the outside world and were completely cut off from humanity during the long dark icy winter. They have left behind photographs and amazing stories - and just as important, the huts where they lived and from which they set out on their great journeys.

What amazing men they were - those early explorers! Ernest Shackleton has always been my favourite - he was such a superb leader when the going got really tough. But all of them were strong and brave men, prepared to put up with enormous discomfort and danger in order to achieve what they regarded as their greatest challenge - indeed their duty!

David Harrowfield knows the Ross Sea and the Antarctic huts well - he has been deeply involved in the repair and maintenance of most of them. This book brings back to life the era of the great Antarctic explorers. The huts on their lonely beaches are living museums of history, adventure and human endeavour. It is important that they be maintained and protected so that future generations can see and admire the resourcefulness and courage of those Antarctic pioneers.

Sir Edmund Hillary, K.G.
Associate Patron, Antarctic Heritage Trust.

Acknowledgements

Antarctic Heritage Trust and the author acknowledge the assistance of many who have helped make this book possible.

The Stout Trust who very generously supplied funds for the writing and printing of the publication.

The initial idea for the book was that of the Trust Chairman, Richard McElrea, with endorsement by the then Patron, Dr Trevor Hatherton. Thanks are also due to Trust personnel Margaret Bradshaw, Harry Burson, Paul Chaplin and Baden Norris for their help and guidance.

Colin Monteath/Hedgehog House New Zealand has generously contributed photographs

The New Zealand Antarctic Programme, particularly Heather Smith, Hellen Robertson and Deidre Sheppard, gave helpful assistance.

Bill Hopper of Wellington willingly provided editorial expertise.

Finally, many Antarctic colleagues of the author, freely made available information and illustrations.

Preface

Early expeditions to the Ross Sea region of Antarctica between 1895 and 1917 - now generally known as the 'heroic-era' of Antarctic exploration - left behind buildings, shelters, camp sites, depots, cairns, message posts, artefacts, memorial crosses and a grave. Similar sites are to be found near the tip of the Antarctic Peninsula and at Commonwealth Bay in East Antarctica. Huts erected on the Shackleton Ice Shelf by Mawson's party (1911-14) and on the Ross Ice Shelf by Amundsen (1910-12) have not been seen since they were abandoned.

Artefacts left from these expeditions form part of the record of early human achievement on the world's harshest continent.

Antarctica is the only continent where the buildings of it's first inhabitants remain, and as such, the early huts are priceless examples of Antarctica's Icy Heritage.

These historic sites were abandoned by the original occupants and owners. They had served their purpose and were left to the elements, and any subsequent expedition that might find them of use.

Since the mid-1950's, these sites have been recognised as places of particular historic interest. Mr L. B. Quartermain MBE, of Wellington wrote several important historical books concerning the expeditions of the 'heroic-era'.

In 1987 the Antarctic Heritage Trust was established in New Zealand to co-ordinate the restoration and on-going protection of the historic sites in the Ross Sea region and to raise funds for this purpose. In 1993 the United Kingdom Antarctic Heritage Trust was also established.

L.B.Quartermain removing ice at Cape Evans 1960-1961. Canterbury Museum

PREFACE

This book records 34 sites which are listed in the Antarctic Heritage Trust Conservation Plan. Most are located in coastal areas from Cape Adare to McMurdo Sound and on Ross Island. Some have not been visited since they were originally abandoned. Because of the diverse activities of the early expeditions, there are numerous other places where traces of human activity have long since disappeared.

These include some of the most historic sites. The depot at Mt Hope, laid by the Ross Sea Party in 1916 has not been seen since. Supply depots variously laid by the Discovery expedition, the Nimrod expedition, the Terra Nova expedition and the Ross Sea Party have long since disappeared under accumulated snow and ice, as have other depots and cairns on the Ross Ice Shelf. With the steady movement of the ice shelf these were destined to ultimately break off in icebergs and eventually fall to the ocean floor.

The historic sites are administered according to the provisions of the Antarctic Treaty 1959, which requires governments to "adopt all adequate measures to protect such tombs, buildings or objects of historic interest from damage or destruction". The Protocol on Environmental Protection to the Antarctic Treaty, Madrid, (1991) forbids the damaging, removal or destruction of historic sites.

A.W Burton NZ Antarctic Society 'caretaker', with a hockey stick and pick found at Cape Evans in 1976-77. NZAP (Neville Peat)

Establishing a Foothold

Due to the often clandestine nature of early sealing and whaling activities in southern waters, it is a matter of conjecture as to which vessel first entered the area now called the Ross Sea. The honour may belong to the British barque, *Venus* under the command of Samuel Harvey, which reached latitude 72°S south in March, 1832.

On New Year's Eve, 1840, Captain James Clark Ross RN, seeking the South Magnetic Pole, rounded the steep volcanic peninsula of Cape Adare. After landing on Possession Islands HMS *Erebus* and HMS *Terror* continued south and on 28 January a 'High Island' was discovered. Ross named the active volcano Erebus, and calculated its height to be 12,400 feet, (3780 metres) just 14 metres short of the mountain's actual height as measured by modern equipment. Other discoveries included "The Barrier" (the Ross Ice Shelf), ' a mighty and wonderful object far beyond anything we could have thought or conceived'.

The first landing on this part of the continent was probably in the area now known as Oates Land, on 26 January 1853, by Mercator Cooper from the American whaling and sealing ship *Levant*. It was followed by Henryk Bull's sealing and whaling expedition in 1894-95 when the *Antarctic* entered the Ross Sea and erected a message post on Svend Foyn Island, one of the Possession Island group. A few days later, on 24 January 1895, a landing was made at Cape Adare.

The Historic Sites

CAPE ADARE AND ROBERTSON BAY

Huts on Ridley Beach at Cape Adare

The Southern Cross and Terra Nova expeditions

Cape Adare, a prominent volcanic headland forming the northern end of the Adare Peninsula, marks the north-east extremity of Victoria Land and the western side of the approaches to the Ross Sea. Discovered by Ross on 11 January 1841, he named it for his friend Viscount Adare, MP for Glamorganshire. From the north end, the peninsula rises to its highest point, Hanson Peak (1256m).

Near the entrance to Robertson Bay, on a shingle beach at the end of the peninsula, are two huts built in 1899 by Carsten Borchgrevink for the Southern Cross expedition. A third hut, now in ruins, was built in 1911 by Lieutenant Victor Campbell, RN, for the Northern Party. Of the three huts, only Borchgrevink's 'living hut' remains in a reasonable state of repair.

Borchgrevink, who had previously landed at Cape Adare from the whaler *Antarctic* in 1895, raised, with the help of British publisher Sir George Newnes, sufficient funds to purchase the former whaling ship *Pollux* and renamed it *Southern Cross*. His ten man shore party became the first group to intentionally winter-over in Antarctica.

The expedition's equipment included two huts of Norwegian spruce. A building (6.4 x 5.5m) for accommodation and a small stores hut (5.35m^2). They also took with them 75 Siberian dogs, two tons of dehydrated food, one ton of Irish butter, 12 gauge paradox guns, .450 calibre Martini-Henry rifles, silk tents, kayaks, aluminium utensils, 53 Primus stoves and 500 miniature Union Jacks," for purposes of survey and extension of the British Empire."

Two days after reaching Cape Adare on 16 February 1899, these stores, together with 400 bags of coal were unloaded on to the beach from the ship's boats.

The huts were constructed of interlocking boards tightened by steel tie rods with the roof of each covered with seal skins weighted down with bags of coal and boulders.

The living hut had its double floor and walls insulated with papier mâché and sliding panels and curtains on the bunks gave some privacy to the occupants. A double-glazed window with an exterior shutter and a saloon lamp from the ship provided lighting. Medical supplies, bottled provisions and surplus clothing were stored in a loft which was later used by Borchgrevink as a study. Two small rooms off the entrance porch were lined with wool and fur and served as a photographic darkroom, instrument storage and for taxidermy. On the windward side, the roof line, which also linked the two buildings, was extended to the ground with spars, sails and seal skins giving additional storage and protection from the weather.

In contrast, the stores hut was a plain, single layered, uninsulated structure.

The *Southern Cross* sailed for New Zealand on 1 March 1899 leaving the ten pioneering explorers to experience man's first planned Antarctic winter.

"At last she was gone," wrote physicist Louis Bernacchi, "and we were alone on that desolate Antarctic shore with nearly 2000 miles of turbulent ocean between us and the nearest inhabited land."

A taste of the violent storms to come was experienced over three days in mid - March when gale-force winds bodily lifted a large whale boat, carrying it 200m out into the ice-strewn sea where it was quickly wrecked.

Life in the living quarters of Camp Ridley was cramped, stuffy and dirty. Severe winter gales demolished the anemometer and removed stones placed around the huts. Large snow drifts on the lee-side gave some protection and it was

The historic huts at Cape Adare soon after construction in late February 1899, made from boards of 40-70 year old Norway spruce.—Eleanor Evans

here that Persen Savio, one of the Lapp dog handlers built a sauna with an iron stove and funnel. The snow drifts also provided kennels for the dogs.

Disaster was never far away from the shore party. While some of the party were away sledging, Nicolai Hanson (zoologist), Kolbein Ellefsen (cook) and Bernacchi, all suffered carbon monoxide poisoning from the coal stove when the wind changed direction while they were asleep. Luckily Bernacchi awoke and was able to throw open the door, allowing fresh air into the room, before falling unconscious across the table.

But the greatest of all calamities to befall the small band of explorers occurred on 14 October, when 28 year old Nicolai Hanson died and became the first person to be buried on the Antarctic continent.

Borchgrevink proposed in the summer to take the stores hut, provisions and a party of four to near either Coulman Island or Cape Gauss and from there, after the winter of 1900, to sledge to the South Magnetic Pole.

Southern Cross returned to Cape Adare on 28 January 1900 and a start was made to dismantle the hut, but at the last minute, for reasons that to this day are not clear, the plan was abandoned. With the wintering party aboard and leaving enough provisions and coal to last another expedition for a year, the ship sailed on 2 February, south, to the edge of the great Ross Ice Shelf before returning to Stewart Island, New Zealand.

On leaving, Bernacchi wrote, "We are not sorry to leave this gelid, desolate spot, our place of abode for so many dreary months. May I never pass such another 12 months in similar surroundings and conditions."

Next to visit Cape Adare, on 8 January 1902, was the Discovery expedition under Commander Robert Falcon Scott RN.

On this occasion Edward Wilson, second surgeon, artist and vertebrate zoologist, wrote,

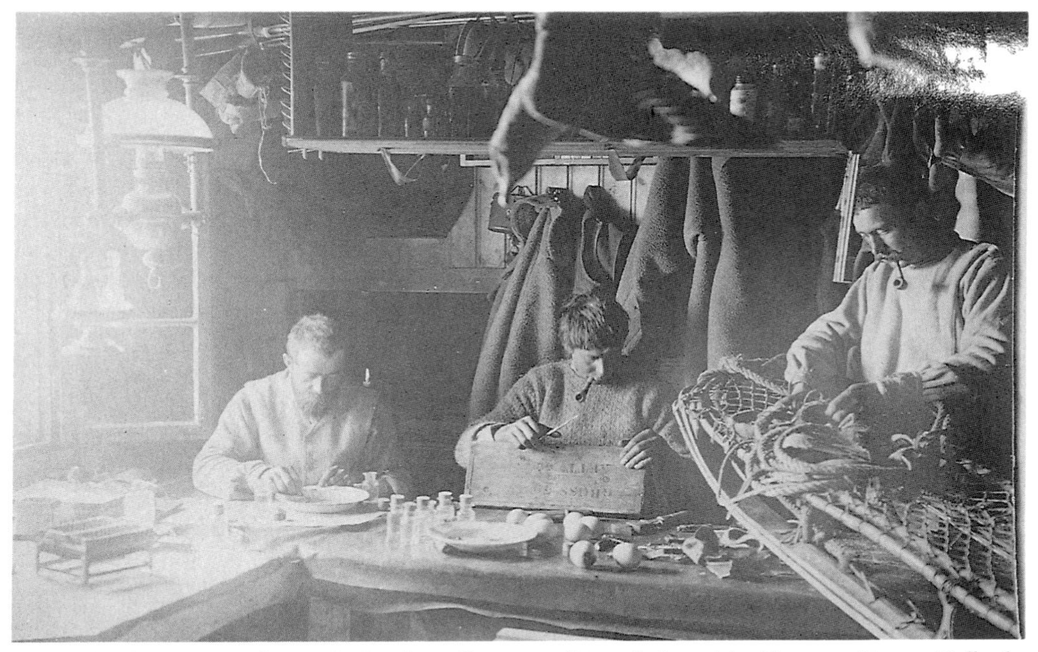

A busy day late in 1899 during the Southern Cross expedition. Left to right: Fougner, Evans, Colbeck.
—Eleanor Evans

"The litter around the huts was very interesting and the waste excessive... the huts looked like the centre of a rubbish heap."

A year later Scott's relief ship, *Morning*, under Captain William Colbeck, formerly of the Southern Cross expedition, also visited the Cape.

The Terra Nova expedition's six member Northern Party (previously designated the Eastern Party), led by Lieutenant Victor Campbell RN arrived at Cape Adare on the morning of 17 February 1911. They had intended to land on King Edward VII Land but their plans were thwarted by heavy pack ice, ice cliffs and the absence of accessible bare rock .

Leading Shipwright Frank Davies RN, the ship's carpenter, found scores of weathered and bleached cases around the huts with no discernible marking to indicate their contents.

"I stuck a pick into one case and found it was ball ammunition," he said, "luckily I did not strike the 'business' end of a cartridge... There was also a solitary dead dog still chained to the wire jackstay."

Although full of stores and snow, both of Borchgrevink's huts were put to good use while the new hut was assembled. Campbell said he liked the design of the Southern Cross hut for a small party, "... although when once ours is up it will be much more palatial." The stores hut, unroofed by Borchgrevink's party on departure, was covered with canvas, partitioned for warmth and had sleeping platforms placed on boxes around two walls. A blubber stove and ice melter were installed and a latrine was built against the outer west wall.

Construction of the 6.35 x 6.15m hut began immediately. Wire ropes over the roof gave additional support. Dried shredded seaweed in hessian quilting provided insulation and a stores annex was built at the east end. A stove was installed for heating and cooking and the completed hut, with one window on the west wall and two on the south, was lit by acetylene. Nearby an ice-house for meat storage was constructed from empty provision cases left by the previous expedition.

Campbell's party experienced similar fierce winds to those recorded by Borchgrevink. On 6 May, the outer wall of the porch made of cases and boards was blown in, but the hut remained intact. Then on 19 June another storm ripped off some of the outer planking. On 3 January 1912 *Terra Nova* picked up the Northern party from Cape Adare.

Norwegian whalers on the chaser *Star 1* viewed the site from offshore in February 1924, and the next recorded visitors were a party landing from the US icebreaker *Edisto* on 9 February 1956. Supplies and equipment from the early expeditions were found scattered over a wide area. The group, wet and cold from landing in a heavy surf, warmed themselves at a fire made from coal briquettes gathered from nearby.

On 14 January 1961, Brian Reid and Colin Bailey of the New Zealand Biological Party landed on Ridley Beach from the US icebreaker *Eastwind* to study the Adélie penguin and skua populations. A few days later, when a storm destroyed their tents, it became necessary to clear ice from Borchgrevink's hut for emergency accommodation.

While they did this, many items were found including seal skins on the floor, a letter to Petty Officer George Abbott RN of the Northern Party, eau de cologne bottles, plum puddings and a biscuit tin from Cape Royds.

On top of Cape Adare, a short distance from Hanson's grave, the party found a tent site marked by basalt boulders, and nearby, under another boulder, a depot containing disintegrated supplies. Before leaving, crew members from the icebreaker assisted with sealing up the hut.

Two other New Zealanders, Shaun Norman and Lawrie Cairns, camped on Ridley Beach between 5 and 9 February 1973. They made emergency repairs to Borchgrevink's hut and transferred the dining table and chairs from the remains of the Northern Party hut. Several artefacts, including an anemometer, a stencilled case with the HMV gramophone dog logo and a harpoon head were recovered and are now in Canterbury Museum.

When the cruise ship *Lindblad Explorer* called at Ridley Beach in January 1974 Antarctic Treaty plaques, in English, French, Russian, and Spanish, were erected by tourists near the huts. This is an example of the cooperation existing between commercial operators and the authorities.

Further repairs and documentation, including a site survey, were undertaken by David Harrowfield, Mark Mabin and Graeme Wilson of the Canterbury Museum Expedition from 9 January to 15 February 1982.

In January 1990, a joint Antarctic Heritage Trust / University of Auckland party of Harrowfield, Gerry Turner, Russell Skerten and Peter Selwyn removed weathered battens and remnants of the original canvas covering from Borchgrevink's living hut. They fastened plywood panels with pre-bonded Butylclad rubber, Balau hardwood ridge cappings and new battens to the roof.

The interior was sprayed with fungicide, the galley area tidied and contents documented. Archival tissue was used to help preserve textiles and papers. The stores hut was excavated by Harrowfield to ascertain the condition of the floor and the site resurveyed. Some artefacts, including the bow of the whale boat wrecked in the March 1899 storm and a sledge were placed in the huts for protection. Other items were removed to New Zealand for conservation by the Trust.

In Borchgrevink's hut is the rusting stove which nearly asphyxiated some of the party and blackened curtaining from the fire in Colbeck's bunk. There are corroding tins of lime juice nodules, dried potato, army rations, Wiltshire bacon, Lea and Perrins sauce and eau de cologne bottles, a kayak frame and hessian dog coats trimmed with red braid.

There is more historic graffiti here than at other sites. Walls and bunks are adorned with signatures and caricatures of expedition members. A fine pencil drawing of a young Scandinavian woman on the ceiling above Ellefsen's bunk has an accompanying sentimental inscription in Norwegian.

"All the bells chime from far away
Tidings from the old days
All the flowers turn and look back with a sigh."

Scattered around outside are roof trusses, wooden barrels, dog tethering pegs with the remains of two dogs still showing yellowish hair, bags of coal, heavy calibre ammunition, a ship's anchor and provision boxes. Traces of the lean-to on the windward side are next to the stores hut, while in the alleyway, is a well-weathered carpenter's bench.

Of the Northern Party hut, only the porch still stands, the walls and roof collapsed, destroyed by gale force winds.

Borchgrevink's living hut is in sound condition, but in contrast, the unroofed stores hut has distorted walls, severe timber weathering at one corner and the floor is buckled and split by the ice beneath.

Another serious problem is the poor condition of artefacts. Iron objects are badly rusted from exposure to salt. The Trust's policy is to return conserved artefacts to the huts, although conditions at Cape Adare may need special consideration.

Today the barren beach of pebbles and penguin guano is much the same as it was in 1899. Post glacial beach ridges are littered with desiccated penguin bodies and there are stagnant lagoons. From off-shore in late summer, when the Adélie rookery is deserted, the bleached huts almost merge with the stark, lonely landscape.

Because of the remoteness of the site and the logistic support required, further work by the Trust can only be accomplished on an 'as opportunity arises' basis. For this reason the Cape Adare site presents special conservation problems.

Hanson's Grave Cape Adare. Southern Cross Expedition

In July 1899 zoologist Nicolai Hanson, who had been unwell on the voyage from England, became ill. His condition deteriorated and in spite of continual attention by Dr Herlof Klovstad he died on the 14 October 1899—the day the Adélie penguins began returning for the summer nesting season.

According to Borchgrevink, Klovstad diagnosed possible "occlusion of the intestines". Some sources suggest the cause of death was either scurvy or beriberi.

Scientific assistant Anton Fougner helped Colbeck make a casket while, at Hanson's dying request, Bernacchi, the dog handler Savio and the other Lapp dog handler Ole Must, used dynamite to excavate a grave on the top of Cape Adare.

Nicolai Hanson c.1898. Photograph made available by his daughter Mrs Johanne Vogt, Norway. —Canterbury Museum.

After a short service in the hut the coffin was pulled up the steep slope with great difficulty.

Hanson's death had a profound effect on his comrades. Their feelings were summed up by Colbeck who said, "We no longer see his cheery face and hear his hearty laugh over the jokes he was so fond of playing on us. The loss to the expedition also as a zoologist is irreparable". Borchgrevink took over the zoological work and Fougner the collection of marine specimens.

When *Southern Cross* returned on 28 January 1900, a grave-side memorial service was held during a snow storm after which a simple black iron cross with an inscribed brass plaque was attached to a large boulder on Hanson's lonely tomb.

Later, when the site served as a lookout for *Terra Nova* in December 1911, Petty Officer Frank Browning RN cleaned and levelled the grave with greenish coloured slabs and black basalt pebbles. He laid out a large cross and the name Hanson with white quartz stones.

The next recorded visitors were Reid and Bailey in January 1960, who found the grave "a lasting affair and in excellent condition."

Sometime later the plaque became detached from the cross and was temporarily wired on by Norman and Cairns in February 1973. It was subsequently found some distance away by Keith Shackleton and Baden Norris from the *Lindblad Explorer* in 1974 and finally re-attached with brass bolts by Harrowfield and Wilson in 1982 who also reformed the pebble inscriptions.

Supply Depot, Ridley Beach, Cape Adare Southern Cross expedition

On the morning of 24 July 1899, Borchgrevink's party suffered a fire that could have had disastrous consequences. As the others slept, Colbeck got up to take scientific observations and while cutting up tobacco let a candle burn too low setting fire to his hair mattress and curtain. Bernacchi later wrote "the paper on the wall caught fire and in a few seconds the whole bunk was wrapped in flame and dense smoke filled the room. Colbeck extinguished the fire but not without considerable difficulty, burning his hands rather badly while doing so."

All that is visible of the depot on Ridley Beach 1982.—David Harrowfield

As a result of this near disaster, ten knapsacks of provisions, one for each member of the party, were prepared and an emergency depot established at the base of the cliffs behind Ridley Beach.

Late in April 1911, geologist Raymond Priestley of the Terra Nova expedition, while walking along the base of the cliffs found the depot and recorded that it, "... had evidently been damaged by rock-falls from the cliff above, but many of the provisions were still in quite good condition."

The next recorded sighting was in January 1982, when Wilson found the handle of a shovel and part of a provision box in guano

View of Ridley Beach from near depot site. Historic huts near seaward end of shingle foreland at centre of photograph, Robertson Bay and the Admiralty Mountains 1982.—David Harrowfield

and debris below a rock overhang. When inspected again in January 1990, little change was apparent.

Supply Depot Cape Adare
Southern Cross expedition

Late in 1899 expedition members frequently climbed to the top of Cape Adare to observe ice conditions and to keep a look out for the *Southern Cross*. Some board fragments, thought to be remains of a depot, were located near the top of the access track in 1982. No trace of the site was found in 1990.

Supply Depot, Cairn and Camp Site
Cape Adare
Terra Nova expedition

After Christmas Day 1911, Victor Campbell decided to maintain a permanent lookout on top of Cape Adare to report on ice conditions and the arrival of *Terra Nova*. A tent was erected in the lee of a huge boulder about 100m east of Hanson's grave, and on 3 January the duty lookout sighted the ship. A depot was left, marked by a rock cairn, and the next day the expedition departed.

Fifty years later, Reid and Bailey, "... found an old food cache approximately 100m N.E. of the grave. None of the food was recognisable as the tins were completely rusted and wafer-thin and many crumbled from handling. The cache, leeward of a large rock, was covered with canvas over which a cairn of stones had been erected. A bamboo marker pole was set in the cairn."

Among the artefacts was a message in a lime juice bottle.

> "This gear was depoted on
> 3rd of January 1912 by the
> Eastern Party of the British
> Antarctic Expedition, while
> looking out for the ship
> Terra Nova, which arrived
> here at 8.30 a.m on the
> 3rd of January 1912."
>
> F.V.Browning"

The camp site by a large boulder on top of Cape Adare in 1911. L-R Browning, Priestley, Dickason.
—R.Priestley

Camp site at Cape Adare marked by boulders used to anchor tent skirt, 1990. Russell Skerten.
—David Harrowfield

Remains of the supply depot at Cape Adare camp site, 1982.—David Harrowfield

The note was eventually given to Dr R.A.Falla, Director, Dominion Museum, Wellington, but its present whereabouts are unknown.

The depot was next visited by Norman and Cairns in 1973, but by 1982 it was in poor condition and the cairn no longer existed.

Harrowfield wrote, " On the ground was a circle of rocks which had been used to weigh down the tent. I measured this at 3.70 - 4m diameter. There were the rotted remains of canvas, a sack with some chaff in it, a bamboo pole (weathered), a sodden, algae coated book of short stories by Mathais McDonnell entitled *Bodkin Q C*, two plain paper note books, several disintegrating tins, a lime juice bottle of paraffin, a rusted tin of cigarettes, a box of Bell's matches, a tin of wax matches, two packets of chocolate and a venesta (plywood) box ." The book and some chocolate were transferred to Borchgrevink's hut.

Little change was seen in the depot in 1990 and the book was returned to New Zealand for conservation by the Antarctic Heritage Trust.

Camp Site, Robertson Bay
Southern Cross expedition

On 22 April 1899, after an aborted attempt to reach the head of Robertson Bay, a refuge camp was established about a metre above the waterline on a crescent shaped shore between Ridley Beach and the Warning Glacier. When the weather deteriorated, the party had time only to rescue some provisions before abandoning the site. An offshore low level helicopter pass in 1982 revealed no trace of it.

Rock Hut, Duke of York Island,
Robertson Bay
Southern Cross expedition

Rising to 470m, Duke of York Island in the south of Robertson Bay is 4 km long, rugged and ice-free. It was first charted by the South-

The rugged eastern coastline of Robertson Bay, 1982. There were few areas along the Adare Peninsula where a camp could be established.—David Harrowfield

The stone hut on Duke of York Island 1899. Borchgrevink (centre rear) farewells Colbeck, Savio (right), and Must (front), as they prepare to leave for Camp Ridley.—C.E.Borchgrevink

The northern side of Duke of York Island 1982 with presumed locality of the stone hut, and to the right, the Murray Glacier.—David Harrowfield

ern Cross expedition in 1899 and named by Borchgrevink for the Duke of York.

Late in July, Borchgrevink accompanied by taxidermist Hugh Evans, dog handlers Must and Savio, with 29 dogs and a month's provisions, sledged across the bay to the island. For shelter they built a 3m diameter rock hut roofed with skis, seal skins, canvas and rocks.

According to Borchgrevink, " The hut was placed in a corner where the rocks of Duke of York Island formed a comparatively sheltered place. It was a cold job. To get the material we had to carry rocks from far off, and break loose pieces off the mountain side. When we had finished we covered it over completely with snow, only leaving a small space open to let the smoke out."

When they left the hut in October, Bernacchi described the scene. "Picture a crude stone hut built of slabs of stone, of sledges, and of tents; in one corner a roaring furnace of seal grease, and seated around, gravely regarding the fire with expressions that would grace a funeral, a group of explorers of so fuliginous and oily appearance as to absolutely defy identification, a perfect sonata in sombre tints, all smoking and blinking in blank contentment."

Scott's Northern Party found no trace of the site in July 1911, nor did a helicopter search by the US icebreaker *Glacier* in 1982.

Supply Depot Crescent Bay, Duke of York Island, Robertson Bay Southern Cross expedition

Crescent Bay, a cove on the north east side of Duke of York Island, was mapped and named, because of its shape by the Southern Cross expedition. It is also the site of a small Adélie penguin rookery.

In late 1899, stores were sledged from Ridley Beach to form a depot. A brief search was made in 1982 but no trace was found.

Crescent Bay, Duke of York Island , site of a small Adélie penguin rookery 1982.—David Harrowfield

Cave, Penelope Point, Robertson Bay
Terra Nova expedition

Penelope Point, a rock headland between the Nielson and Scott Keltie Glaciers on the west side of Robertson Bay, was first mapped by the Northern Party, and named for Terra Nova's master, Lieutenant Harry Pennell RN whose nickname was "Penelope".

Like Borchgrevink, the Northern Party was limited in the exploration and science it could carry out in the Robertson Bay area, but in September 1911, a number of sledging trips were made while the sea was frozen. A deep cave was found by Campbell, Priestley, Browning, Abbott and Able Seaman Harry Dickason RN.

"12.30. Lunched in a large cave just north of a prominent cape," wrote Campbell. "The cave, which was 82 yards long, had a beautiful 'Norman' entrance, the layers of quartz and green slate of which the cliff is formed giving it a very fine appearance."

After spending several nights in the 'Abbey Cave', the party depoted two week's provisions with a sledge and continued north along the coast to Cape Wood. Here a depot was left for a future journey. On their return they again camped in the cave.

"It was on this occasion," said Priestley, " that the 'Abbey Cave' got its name for the roof and sides acted like great sounding boards, and our usual Sunday concert sounded quite impressive."

The final visit was made during the second western journey on 4 October, when a sledge and two week's provisions were cached.

The cave was not revisited until Harrowfield, Turner, Skerten and Selwyn camped at Cape Adare in 1989-90. A helicopter sighting on 31 December revealed the interior to contain only blocks of ice.

Camp outside the 'Abbey Cave', Penelope Point, 1911.—R.Priestley.

The cave at Penelope Point 31 December 1989. Using a copy of the historic photograph the helicopter pilots from the US icebreaker Polar Star *were able to locate the cave with little difficulty.*
—Gerry Turner.

Antarctic's *message post when visited by the Southern Cross expedition in 1900.—C.E.Borchgrevink*

View of Svend Foyn Island, site of an Adélie penguin rookery, from the tourist ship Frontier Spirit *15 February 1993. Because of heavy sea ice a landing was not made.—David Harrowfield*

POSSESSION ISLANDS

Message Post, Svend Foyn Island

Norwegian Sealing and Whaling expedition

Svend Foyn, also known as Foyn Island, lies some 6km south west of Possession Island. It is the largest in the group and was named in 1895 by Henryk Bull and Captain Leonard Kristensen of the *Antarctic* after Norwegian whaler Svend Foyn, owner of the ship and primary financier of the expedition.

On 16 January 1900, a landing party, including Borchgrevink, erected a pole with a box attached containing Kristensen's card. The ship then continued south to Coulman Island before returning to Cape Adare.

The post was discovered intact by the Southern Cross expedition on 3 February 1900.

"The paper was found in the tobacco box nailed to the post and in a perfect state of preservation," said Bernacchi. "The letter was short and merely stated that the ship *Antarctic*, Captain Kristensen, had called here on the 18th of January, 1895. After having placed a penciled note signed by each member of the party in the tin box, it was again secured."

The marker post, still vertical, was sighted from the US icebreaker *Edisto* in 1956 and again from the US icebreaker *Glacier* in 1965. Its condition is unknown.

COULMAN ISLAND

Message Post, Cape Wadworth

Discovery expedition

Ross discovered Cape Wadworth, the northern extremity of Coulman Island, on 17 January 1841 naming it for his wife's uncle, Robert John Coulman of Wadworth Hall, Doncaster, but the first landing was made by Borchgrevink on 4 February 1900.

On 15 January 1902 while *Discovery* was

View of Cape Wadworth, Coulman Island and the emperor penguin rookery. The island is volcanic and largely ice covered.—Colin Monteath / Hedgehog House New Zealand.

searching for winter quarters, Scott landed on Cape Wadworth and nailed a metal cylinder to a red pole about 8m above sea level and to make it more conspicuous, painted the rocks behind it red and white. The next known sighting of the post was when Andy Brown, a pilot with Helicopters New Zealand, visited the area during the summer of 1989-90. The post was not examined and its condition is unknown.

TERRA NOVA BAY

Site of Ice Cave, Inexpressible Island

Terra Nova expedition

Only 11km long, Inexpressible Island, which forms the west shore of Evans Cove in Terra Nova Bay, is one of the most important historic sites in the Ross Sea region. Originally named Southern Foothills by the Northern

Priestley at the entrance to the ice cave on Inexpressible Island after the winter of 1912.—R.Priestley

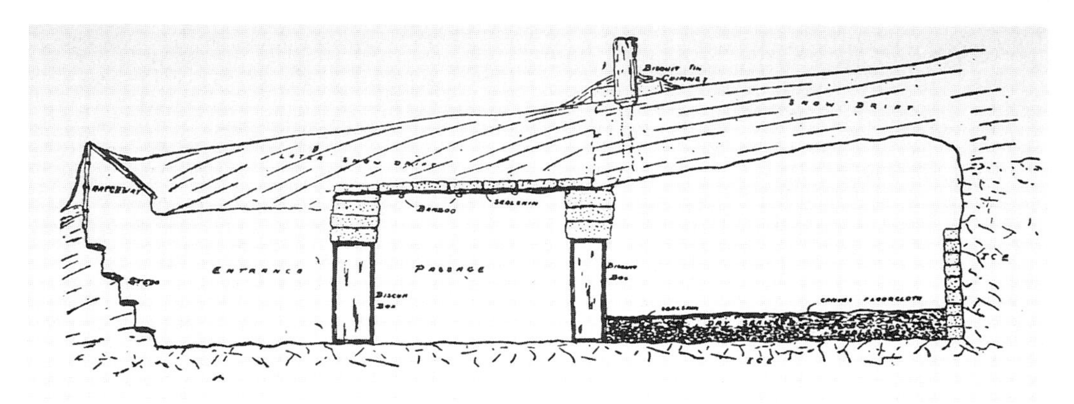

Section through the ice cave after a drawing by R. Priestley.

Site of ice cave entrance on Inexpressible Island, in 1962-63 with bamboos and part of seal skin roof lining visible.—NZAP(David Skinner)

Party, it was the setting for an uncomfortable winter on half rations for them in 1912.

After wintering at Cape Adare, Campbell's six man party embarked on *Terra Nova* on 4 January and sailed south to Evans Cove where a depot was placed.

With supplies limited to six weeks' sledging rations, two weeks 'pemmican and about four weeks' of other food they attempted to carry out further geological exploration, but little progress was made because of the difficult terrain, and having failed to reach Wood Bay, the party returned to Inexpressible Island.

It was approaching autumn, and because of heavy pack ice,*Terra Nova* was unable to pick them up. Fearing something had happened to the ship, and with their two tents badly damaged by wind, Campbell decided to excavate a cave. Set in a snow covered ice bank, it was only 3.6 x 2.7m, and less than 1.7m high.

For insulation, the cavern was lined with snow blocks and the ice floor covered with gravel and seaweed topped with tent floor cloths and seal skins. The entrance was a 'torpedo hatch' made from biscuit boxes. There was an inner and outer galley, two sack curtains to prevent smoke and draughts, a biscuit tin chimney and a bamboo ventilator. The roof was lined with seal skins supported by bamboos.

The party moved in on 17 March with a stock of penguin and seal meat to supplement their meagre supplies. Adhering to British Naval tradition, an imaginary line separated officers from men and under these extraordinary conditions, with barely enough room to crouch, they were forced to spend the winter.

"From amid the smoke which arises from the cheery blubber fire the blackened oven looms dimly, its squat body supported by bamboo uprights from which are slung penguins, a seal's head, and huge joints of red meat," wrote Raymond Priestley. "... Levick crouches near the fire and stirs the hoosh and as he swirls it

The ice cave site at Inexpressible Island, February 1984.—Colin Monteath / Hedgehog House New Zealand

Looking towards Terra Nova Bay and Drygalski Ice Tongue left, December 1971. Country familiar to the Northern Party.—Richard McElrea

round and round a most appetising smell arises." Hoosh was a soup like stew.

But, even Priestley's picturesque description could not dispel the bouts of depression brought on by hunger, poor hygiene, cold and the cave's gloom that plagued its occupants.

Then in late September, and without having washed for nine months, the six weary men drew lots for clean clothes, and began a gruelling 40-day, 370km trek south along the coast. Supplies cached at Depot Island, Cape Roberts and Butter Point proved to be their salvation. Tired and filthy the party reached the comparative safety of Hut Point on 6 November. It was there they learned of Scott's death.

Terra Nova revisited the site on 25 January 1913 at the close of the expedition, enabling crew to gather mementoes of this 'unparalleled habitation'.

The next recorded visit to Inexpressible Island was 25 January 1963, by the New Zealand Geological and Topographical Antarctic Expedition.

"On moving south and west around the westernmost tip of the island, we entered a small inlet and were here thrilled to find - about 200 yards from the beach - in one of the few snow drifts, the remains of the snow cave in which the Northern Party of 1912 had spent the long Antarctic winter," wrote leader and surveyor Ron Hewson.

He also found bamboo poles covered with seal skins that formed the roof to the entrance tunnel. A small blubber stove and a blubber lamp made from a biscuit tin, and, under a large rock nearby had been stuffed a blubbery set of windproof clothing along with a few old gloves, socks and puttees.

Inexpressible Island has been visited by scientists during the summers of 1964-65, 1969-70, 1981-82, 1982-83, in 1984-85 when Antarctic Treaty plaques were installed, 1989-90, 1993-94 and in 1994-95.

A visit in December 1982 revealed the site to be obscured by snow, but when inspected on 7 December 1985, ablation had destroyed the cave. Laurie Greenfield and Trevor Chinn reported numerous artefacts amongst the large granite boulders, and a proliferation of cut and blackened penguin and seal bones scattered by the north-east katabatic winds.

On instructions from Bob Thomson, then Director, New Zealand Antarctic Research Programme, items of clothing, three blubber stoves, *Reviews of Reviews*- one of two books with Campbell's party - and other artefacts, were returned to Scott Base for protection. Unfortunately all but two of these historic items linked to one of Antarctica's greatest exploits were lost while awaiting return to New Zealand for conservation. Only two gloves, and the book, which will be conserved by the Antarctic Heritage Trust, survive.

Supply Depot, Hells Gate Moraine, Inexpressible Island Terra Nova expediton

The glacial moraine at Hell's Gate is located at the head of Evans Cove on the coast of northern Victoria Land and extends south to Hell's Gate from nearby Vegetation Island and Cape Confusion. It was mapped and named by the Northern Party in association with Hell's Gate, a narrows near the east edge of the Nansen Ice Sheet. Evans Cove was discovered by *Nimrod* while searching for the Magnetic Pole party in 1909.

On arriving at Evans Cove on 8 January 1912, four days after leaving Cape Adare, the crew of *Terra Nova* assisted Campbell to establish a depot on a moraine, first called Depot Moraine, but later renamed Hell's Gate Moraine. Two weeks' pemmican for six men, three 56 lb boxes of sugar, 24 lb of cocoa, 36 lb of chocolate, and five 42 lb cases of biscuit were left with spare clothes, bamboos and sufficient equipment for six weeks' sledging. It was designed to provide security if *Terra Nova* was unable to return and pick them up. In the event it was not used.

The next morning, after securing the depot, the group began sledging. They returned 20 days later and a party under Dr Murray Levick

Depot site at Hell's Gate Moraine January 1994. The depot was between two large boulders (centre) on edge of moraine.—ICAIR (Colin Harris)

was sent to Hell's Gate depot to await the ship. To their surprise, Frank Debenham's party, which was supposed to arrive from Granite Harbour, had not been landed and, "our letters to him still being in the 'post box' we had fixed up." By 1 March, when it became clear that the ship might not arrive, preparations began for wintering. Four days later it was decided to start digging an ice cave for winter quarters, and some supplies were retrieved from the depot. On 12 April bamboos, oil, and a blubber chopping board were uplifted. Further supplies were obtained on 13 August when a note was left, " in case a relief party should by any chance come from the Wood Bay area."

In readiness for the spring journey back to Cape Evans, more supplies were collected from the depot and Priestley's rock specimens cached.

When *Terra Nova* called on 25 January 1913, at the conclusion of the expedition, Priestley's specimens were recovered. The depot was stocked and marked by a bamboo and flag was left.

While making geological observations and counting seals along the western shore of the island adjacent to Hell's Gate on 25 January 1963, surveyor Ron Hewson and his party stumbled across the food depot put ashore by *Terra Nova* exactly fifty years previously. Along with six weeks' rations for six men, the cache contained a Nansen man-hauling sledge, a 120 foot climbing rope, a Nansen-type combination cooker, a polar tent, and a pick and shovel.

"The food (oatmeal, sugar, cocoa, biscuits) was all contained in large soldered tins and, except for one damaged tin of biscuits which we opened, all was left exactly as it was when found. The wooden sledge and cane tent poles had all been extensively weathered while the rope and tent were still complete but very rotten," wrote Hewson.

The depot was examined by Graeme

Attaching panels to roof of Borchgrevink's living hut in January 1990. Gerry Turner (L) and Russell Skerten (on roof).—David Harrowfield

Borchgrevink's living hut February 1995.—NZAP (Tim Higham)

The galley area of Borchgrevink's living hut 1990.—David Harrowfield

Medical supplies from the Southern Cross expedition, January 1982.—David Harrowfield

Pencil sketch of Scandinavian woman, above Ellefsen's bunk, January 1990, Southern Cross expedition. —David Harrowfield

Hut erected by Scott's Northern Party in 1911, for the second wintering at Cape Adare.—R. Priestley

Remains of the Northern Party hut February 1994. The building is now beyond repair.—NZAP (Emma Waterhouse)

Hanson's lonely grave on the summit of Cape Adare 1982. Mark Mabin. —David Harrowfield

The Discovery expedition winter quarters and McMurdo Station. The tourist vessel Lindblad Explorer *is at the ice wharf in Winter Quarters Bay.—Colin Monteath / Hedgehog House New Zealand.*

Exterior of Discovery hut August 1990.—NZAP (Kim Westerskov)

Interior of Discovery hut December 1989 with blubber stove (1911) and sleeping platforms used by Ross Sea Party.—NZAP (Chris Rudge)

Discovery hut with McMurdo Sound and Royal Society Range in background 1994.—Ed Anderson

View of the interior with galley to right, at Cape Royds.—Colin Monteath / Hedgehog House New Zealand

"Vince's Cross" on Hut Point.—NZAP (Malcolm Macfarlane)

Shackleton's hut at Cape Royds and Mt Erebus 1994.—Ed Anderson.

Lubricant for the Arrol Johnston motor car, Cape Royds.—Colin Monteath / Hedgehog House New Zealand

View of Cape Evans historic site and Barne Glacier—Colin Monteath / Hedgehog House New Zealand

The galley, or kitchen, at Cape Evans, 1994.—Ed Anderson

Scientific glassware in the laboratory, Cape Evans.—NZAP (Chris Rudge)

A view towards the "Wardroom" at Cape Evans.—NZAP (Shaun Norman)

Ponting's darkroom, Cape Evans hut, also used by Spencer-Smith of the Ross Sea Party.—Colin Monteath / Hedgehog House New Zealand

Victoria Land coast from the summit of Mount England with the Mackay Glacier beyond.—Colin Monteath / Hedgehog House New Zealand

The supply depot on Hell's Gate Moraine January 1994—ICAIR (Colin Harris)

Claridge and Iain Campbell of the New Zealand Soil Bureau in December 1964, and by David Skinner's NZARP party in January 1970, when the depot was found intact, "...although the Nansen cooker appears to have been used and put back unwashed, and food boxes, other than the biscuits opened in 1963, have had the sides opened to get at the contents."

Skinner, Norman, Colin Brodie and Chris Morris while mapping for the New Zealand Geological Survey - DSIR Terra Nova Bay Expedition, visited Hell's Gate Moraine on 26 December 1982 to find that three inches of pick axe handle and the corner of a food box were the only indications that something lay beneath the snow. The cache was cleared, individual items put in the sun to dry and artefacts listed.

Skinner noted, "Everything is in an advanced state of decay due to 70 years of wind blast, salt spray, penguins, rust and perhaps tourists. Much of this decay has been since 1970. I believe that unless the cache is soon removed to New Zealand for limited restoration and use in displays, it will be a pile of rust, sticks and old bits of rope and leather in a very few years. On leaving, we repacked it with stones to hold everything down and marked the boulder next to it with a small cairn."

Although the site is often concealed by snow, the Antarctic Heritage Trust recommended in October 1988 that the sledge and Nansen cooker be removed to ensure their preservation. However when visited that summer by GANOVEX Expedition geologists, the cache was not visible. Inspected again in January 1994, the contents of the depot, which appeared to be in two caches, was listed. The Trust recommended all artefacts be removed for conservation and this was carried out by Neville Ritchie and Roger Fyfe with assistance of the New Zealand Antarctic Programme in January 1995.

HUT POINT, ROSS ISLAND

Building, Hut Point

Discovery expedition

Hut Point, Ross Island, is a small volcanic promontory about one and a half kilometres north west of Cape Armitage which lies at the south end of Hut Point Peninsula. It was named by the Discovery expedition which established their shore station there.

Exploration and scientific observations as well as reaching the South Pole were the primary objectives of the expedition which was equipped with the new 52.4m barque-rigged steamer, *Discovery*. Provisions for three years for the 48 men, 32 of whom were from the Royal Navy, included 42,000 lbs flour, 10,000 lb sugar, 3000 lb roast beef, 800 gallons of rum and 45 live sheep. Reindeer and wolfskin suits, a windmill to power a dynamo for electric light, two tethered balloons and 23 sledge dogs were also offloaded.

After failing to find a suitable site in King Edward V11 Land, Scott decided to winter in Ross's 'McMurdo Bay' (McMurdo Sound). Mooring the ship on the south side of Hut Point on 9 February 1902, preparations immediately began for wintering with an awning being fitted over part of the upper deck, while about 200m away the frozen ground was excavated for the foundations of a 9.3 x 9.1m wooden building bought in Australia for £360.14s.5d.

Similar in design to Australian outback houses, the prefabricated building was intended to accommodate the landing party and to provide shelter should *Discovery* be driven from her moorings. It had a verandah around three sides and double thickness walls and floor insulated with felt. Seven double glazed windows in three walls and six skylights with shutters provided lighting. Electric power was originally envisaged but not installed.

After completion, the building was painted terra-cotta but the difficulty of maintaining a comfortable temperature and the need to conserve coal, resulted in it not being used for accommodation. Expedition members remained on the ship, where in spite of dampness and the formation of ice in the cabins, most occupants were fairly comfortable and contented.

Nearby, two small wood-framed, asbestos-clad huts, were erected for Louis Bernacchi's observations in magnetism and seismology.

The shore station was used to dry furs and tents after sledging, for skinning birds, as a repair shop and as a venue for entertainments. It was known as 'Gregory Lodge' for Professor J.W.Gregory FRS, who was originally appointed by the Royal Society as leader of the scientific staff, but who resigned to take up a position at Melbourne University before *Discovery* sailed. It was also called 'The Royal Terror Theatre'.

The building gained greater importance during the later expeditions of Lieutenant Ernest Shackleton RNR and Scott.

In 1908 the Nimrod party gained entry through a window and found the interior to be largely snow free. They made great use of the building, partitioning it with boxes of provisions for warmth.

On his second expedition, Scott intended using the building for a wintering party in 1911, but sea ice prevented *Terra Nova* getting close enough to offload stores. In March 1911, a depot laying party cleared the accumulated ice and again re-partitioned the building with cases. A brick blubber-burning stove was constructed, asbestos sheets were obtained from the collapsed magnetic huts to level the floor and the verandah on the south side enclosed to form stables.

Extensive use of the building was made by the Ross Sea Party in 1915-16. Dog handler, Victor Hayward observed, "there was a fair quantity of grub and plenty of cigars". Also souvenired were one and a half bottles of Crème de Menthe, two sleeping bags, and a pair of Wolseys (presumably "long johns") belonging to Captain Lawrence Oates, 6th Innskilling Dragoons, which were given to the Reverend Arnold Spencer-Smith.

With the autumn depot laying over, early

Building of the Discovery expedition, magnetic huts, the ship Discovery, *and surrounding landscape of Winter Quarters Bay in 1902. —R.Skelton. Canterbury Museum*

April 1915 found members of the Ross Sea Party in residence waiting for the sea ice to become firm enough for their return to Cape Evans. "Meals somehow seem to be the principal event of the day," wrote their leader, Lieutenant Aeneas Mackintosh RNR. "Before one is prepared it's discussed and gone into thoroughly." A few days later when their stock of candles ran out he noted, "... the improvised blubber lamps are in full swing. The smoke though is terrific, we breath it and our clothes are practically oozing with blubber." As a consequence, the building became blackened with soot.

The Ross Sea Party again occupied the building from mid-March until mid-July 1916. At the end of June, when low on seal blubber, they began to chop up part of the building for fuel.

Their place of refuge was half filled with snow and many days were spent huddled about the brick blubber stove, illuminated only by the red glow of the hot plate and the flickering light from blubber lamps made from old tins. As blubber melted onto the floor, it was scraped up and reburned and in physicist Dick Richard's words, "It may have been a dark cheerless place, but to us it represented security. We lived the life of troglodytes. We slept in our clothes in old sleeping bags which rested on planks raised above the floor by wooden provision cases."

For the next thirty years the building stood solitary and silent, filled with ice until visited by the US ice breaker *Burton Island* on 20 February 1947. Scattered outside were pony snow shoes, skis, sledges, mutton carcasses, a hitching rail and cases of supplies.

With the establishment in the summer of 1955-56 of the Air Operations Facility of Operation Deep Freeze 1, a tent camp was set up adjacent to 'Gregory Lodge'. Dog kennels, the foundations of the two magnetic huts, the remains of a heating stove, a humidifier, sledges, mutton carcasses and a flag pole were among the artefacts still to be found laying about the building.

In January 1956 some 90 assorted artefacts including provisions, a sledge, sleeping bag, thermometer, and harpoon from the huts at Hut Point, Cape Evans and Cape Royds were taken to England by Lt.Cdr. Michael J. Foster RN, a UK observer with Operation Deep Freeze.

The flag pole was retrieved in 1955-56 and later presented to Sir Edmund Hillary to stand in front of New Zealand's newly built Scott Base as a memorial to the base's namesake and his comrades who endured so much during the early days of Antarctic exploration.

As the forerunner to McMurdo Station expanded, the US commander, Rear Admiral George Dufek USN, decreed that the historic building was to be treated as a shrine and monument to human endeavour and prohibited his men going near it or taking anything from it. This status was also extended to the huts at Cape Evans and Cape Royds.

By now moves were well underway to preserve the historic sites with Arthur Helm, Secretary to the Ross Sea Committee of the Commonwealth Trans-Antarctic Expedition 1955-58 (TAE), and of the New Zealand Antarctic Society, urging immediate action. But restoration work on the sites at Cape Evans and Cape Royds in the summer of 1960-61 came first and it was not until later that the New Zealand and United States Antarctic Treaty Consultative Committee Members agreed that steps should be taken to restore the Discovery hut.

A restoration party of Eric Gibbs, Baden Norris, Rodney Smith and Grant Hurrell, all volunteers from the New Zealand Antarctic Society, began work in January 1964. They entered the building through the door on the south side and, as years of accumulated ice was removed, many poignant links with the past were uncovered with details being recorded by Smith and Norris.

There was an original script for the comedy, *Ticket of Leave* performed in 1902, letters written by Mackintosh and Ernest Joyce (a general hand with the Ross Sea Party), improvised sleeping platforms, emperor penguin skins, ten chess men carved from a broom handle, desiccated oranges, and from behind the blubber stove, some scones. After a month, the building was sealed with tarpaulins until work could be completed the following summer.

Later 'Hut caretakers' of the New Zealand Antarctic Society carried out valuable work until the formation of the Historic Sites Management Committee (HSMC) an advisory committee of the Ross Dependency Research Committee (RDRC). In 1987, the Antarctic Heritage Trust's conservation programme began, and since then, Scott Base winter-over staff have assisted in maintaining the building and clearing infiltrating snow.

Annual building deformation surveys undertaken by the Department of Survey and Land Information (DOSLI) have confirmed Rodney Smith's 1964 observations that the building is settling unevenly causing bowing of walls away from the floor and movement of the verandah. This major concern of the Trust's Conservation Advisory Group (CAG) may be due to changes in local permafrost or the effect of vehicle movement on the foundations. However, given its age, with the exception of some interior floor damage, cracked glass skylights and extensive weathering and shrinkage of the roof cladding, the building is relatively sound and the Trust has recommended that any future work should be done with minimal alteration to the original appearance.

While the Trust has collected some environmental data, there is a need for more detailed information on temperature and relative humidity levels. Light levels, detrimental to artefacts, are fortunately low. In 1986 a selection of artefacts was removed from the hut to be conserved.

The Discovery hut is the most accessible of all the 'heroic-era' structures as it stands close to the United States' McMurdo scientific and logistic complex. As a result, it receives the greatest number of visitors, with several hundred being recorded by the Trust each year. As with the other historic sites, the building is kept locked. There is a Code of Conduct for visitors which restricts visitor numbers, handling of artefacts, smoking and the presence of naked flames.

Because of the building's popularity as a recreational resource, the Trust recognises the need for detailed supplementary management plans that will include the sensitive provision of interpretative materials. Fyfe, has suggested that owing to the paucity of artefacts, visitor centre type didactic displays would help to enlighten and illustrate the 'heroic-era'. This could be supplemented by the establishment of a Ross Island Heritage Centre enabling many more people to gain an appreciation of the historic sites and to take visitor pressure off Hut Point. Ritchie, also recommends the creation of an 'historic precinct' around the site including the eventual removal of equipment used to support McMurdo Station. The Trust has yet to formally decide on these measures.

Winter Quarters Bay today presents a different setting to the one encountered by Scott in 1902. Surrounding slopes are dominated by McMurdo Station, the largest base on the continent. Discovery hut and the near-by memorial cross to Able Seaman George Vince seem almost out of place. While the climate has weathered the old building, it still has traces of terra-cotta paint and the coded inscriptions for assembling. Part of Discovery's awning, a seal carcass, and a few provision boxes, are all that lie in the scoria outside. No trace remains of the dog lines, the hitching rail, or kennels that were present in 1956 and the whereabouts of many other artefacts is a mystery. The remains of the magnetic huts were salvaged by the 1963-64 restoration party and have been put inside Discovery hut.

Inside are stark reminders of all the expeditions that used the building. Brick foundations for Bernacchi's gravity instrument, provisions from Cape Royds, tent poles and the blubber stove installed during the Terra Nova expedition. There are the Ross Sea Party's primitive blubber lamps made from split pea tins, their sleeping platforms and improvised clothing fashioned from tent canvas and sleeping bags. Damage to flooring and the inner ceiling is evidence of their chopping up seals and removing timber for fuel. The building is cold and with the pervading aroma of seal meat and blubber, it exudes an unforgettable atmosphere of the hardships encountered by the early explorers.

The sediment on the sea-bed of Winter Quarters Bay doubtless hides many artefacts linked with *Discovery* including the leg irons thrown over board by the cook in 1902, but in spite of an extensive search by US Navy divers in 1964, nothing from the ship has been found.

But what of Scott's ship? After serving Sir Douglas Mawson's 1929-31 British Australian New Zealand Antarctic Research Expedition (BANZARE) the 700 ton polar veteran *Discovery* is now being restored at its birthplace in Scotland by the Dundee Heritage Trust.

Vince's Cross, Hut Point
Discovery expedition

Danger, sometimes ending with death, has been a constant companion for all who venture into Antarctica and on Ross Island several memorial crosses have been erected to commemorate those who died while exploring the great white unknown.

In March 1902, a sledging party set out for Cape Crozier to change the message left there for the relief ship, *Morning*. On the 11th, during their return journey, they were engulfed by a blizzard near Castle Rock and a fatal mistake was made in trying to reach *Discovery*. Able Seaman George Vince, wearing finnesko (fur boots) lost his footing on the icy surface and slid over an ice cliff into the freezing sea at Danger Slopes. He was not seen again.

As a memorial to the first man to die in McMurdo Sound, Vince's shipmates erected a white painted hardwood cross overlooking the sea at Hut Point just 100m from the Discovery hut.

The cross, a mute reminder of the vulnerability of life in Antarctica, has been blown over on a number of occasions, the last time during the winter of 1987. Because of hillside erosion it has been repositioned slightly, a concrete base attached and a new section of oak fitted by Scott Base carpenters Mike McGuinn and Dean Christie. The cross is in good condition and the carved inscription is quite legible.

Sacred
To The Memory of
George. T. Vince
A.B. R.N.
Of The
"Discovery"
Who was drowned near this spot.
March 11th 1902

CAPE ROYDS, ROSS ISLAND

Building, Cape Royds

Nimrod expedition

Cape Royds, a volcanic headland, forms the western extremity of Ross Island facing McMurdo Sound and was named by the Discovery expedition for its meteorologist, Lieutenant Charles Royds RN. A camp was established on the Cape while a lookout was being maintained for the relief ship *Morning* in 1903-04.

In late January 1908, Ernest Shackleton in *Nimrod*, like Scott before him, was unable to land in King Edward V11 Land and decided to enter McMurdo Sound. With local ice conditions preventing him from reaching Hut Point, Cape Royds was chosen as the site to establish the expedition's winter quarters.

A start was made on 6 February to erect a 7 x 8.5m prefabricated building bought in London for £154. Foundations were dug in the rocky, frozen ground and wooden piles set with a mixture of cement and cinders. The unpainted building was insulated with Stoniflex felt and granular cork, helped by stacking stores around the south-east and south walls. The 30cm space between the walls and cased provisions was filled with gravel. A seven-light carbide acetylene generator was installed, and two double glazed windows fitted in the north wall. Although two stoves were provided, only the large American, 'Mrs Sam' Columbian range was used. The other, was of French manufacture and fitted with a hot water tank.

Stables were added along the north wall for the four surviving Manchurian ponies (of the 10 taken on board *Nimrod*, 2 were shot on the ship and 4 died at Cape Royds) and a garage built for the 12-15 hp Arrol-Johnston car, the first motor transport used in Antarctica.

Except for Shackleton, who had his own 'room', expedition members were accommodated in two-man cubicles with improvised beds and duck curtains hanging from wires. Artist George Marston painted panels of Joan of Arc at the stake and Napoleon, on his curtains, while surgeon and cartographer, Eric Marshall furnished his space with a table made out of wash-basin legs and a drawing board. Two other small rooms became a laboratory and photographic darkroom.

Shackleton wrote, "It was not a very spacious dwelling for the accommodation of fifteen persons, but our narrow quarters were warmer than if the hut had been larger."

When members of the Terra Nova expedition first visited Cape Royds in January 1911 they found evidence of a rapid departure. A meal was on the table and socks were hung on a line to dry.

Cape Royds was also visited by members of the Ross Sea Party during 1915-16 who foraged for matches, tobacco and soap and collected biological specimens left by the previous occupants.

When the US ice breaker *Edisto* arrived 29 January 1948, boards were missing from the roof, the stables were full of snow and the garage had collapsed. Maize kernels, collected by Captain John Cadwalader USN, were later germinated in the United States. Commander David Nutt visiting the site found that nails from a broken keg laying outside the hut were as good as the day they were made and showed only a few rust spots.

A convivial gathering at Cape Royds 1908. Ernest Joyce in centre.—Canterbury Museum.

The Arrol-Johnston car outside the garage at Cape Royds, 1908.—Canterbury Museum

Shackleton's hut at Cape Royds 1908.—Canterbury Museum.

In 1957 and again in 1958 crew from HMNZS *Endeavour* carried out much clearing, cleaning and general maintenance on both the Cape Royds and Cape Evans huts.

A Huts Restoration Committee, established in 1959, comprised of representatives from Government and the New Zealand Antarctic Society, recommended that the building be returned to its original state. The main aims were to stop further deterioration, prevent pilfering and vandalism and to retrieve and preserve all artefacts of value.

In Leslie Quartermain's words, "The hut interiors we propose to restore as nearly as possible to the appearance they had when occupied; not looking like museum pieces, ticketed and labelled, but giving the impression that the occupants have just moved out. We don't plan any major reconstruction work, but aim to make the buildings weatherproof without interfering with their original appearance."

From December 1960 to January 1961, Quartermain's party toiled to restore the building which was very dirty both inside and out. The only areas able to be brought back to their original appearance were the biological laboratory and adjoining cook's store where a notice was found instructing visitors to :

"Please leave
the dishes clean.
The hungry man
coming in needs
them. He is empty.
You are leaving
with a full belly."

Outside, garage walls were reconstructed and the stable de-iced. Objects located included experimental wheels for the Arrol-Johnston car, pony harness, a dredge with Professor David's name on it, and a man-haul sledge retrieved from Pony Lake.

In November 1969, the first New Zealand Antarctic Society 'hut caretakers', Peter Skellerup (later inaugural Chairman of Antarctic Heritage Trust) and Michael Orchard worked at Cape Royds. Finding Shackleton's signature was a highlight. "Went and got my torch to look at Shackleton's wee bunkroom and saw his signature on the head-end of his wooden bunk," wrote Skellerup.

Later 'caretaker' maintenance parties discovered many interesting artefacts. In 1972 Varian Wilson and Peter Wilson located one of the experimental wheels in Pony Lake with the second wheel and the front ski being recovered by Gordon Sylvester and Ken Smith in 1974. A detailed building report was prepared by John Oliver in 1979 providing guidelines for future work.

Antarctic Heritage Trust activities at Cape Royds began in 1987 and have included compiling architectural drawings, sorting disintegrating stores, collecting environmental data, listing artefacts and general maintenance.

In 1990 a Butylclad rubber sheathing was attached to the gambrel roof by a Trust party led by Rodger Cullen assisted by a youth group. The new covering replaced painted canvas railway tarpaulins fitted in 1960. Further roof maintenance and window replacement was undertaken by John Charles' team in 1991-92 and 1992-93.

In general, the building is in good condition but concern by conservators at the state of tinned provisions and other artefacts has led the Trust to install a data logger to monitor temperature and relative humidity. A detailed inventory of over 2000 artefacts has been com-

The weather station, outside Shackleton's winter quarters at Cape Royds.—David Harrowfield

The remains of a supply depot at Back Door Bay in 1971. This has since almost disappeared.Harry Burson at Cape Royds.—Richard McElrea

pleted and ranked according to conservation requirements.

With the building now snow-free, the greatest concern is for stores stacked outside, especially along the south-east and south walls. In spite of restacking, restrapping and removal of those that are in the worst condition, deterioration is accelerating. To ensure their preservation, they will require further sorting and repackaging with the discarding of non-essential material. A stores area could be recreated and an archaeological investigation made of the historic rubbish dump.The Heritage Management Plan sets guidelines and defines what is considered 'historic rubbish'.

Within the Cape Royds hut well-presented static displays will form part of an important curatorial and museological programme for the Trust.

Cape Royds is perhaps one of the most beautiful and fascinating places in Antarctica. From the hut's door can be seen the world's most southern Adélie penguin rookery and the wild grandeur of the Transantarctic Mountains, while from of a low volcanic ridge behind, a spectacular panorama unfolds -- Mt Erebus, Cape Barne, the Barne Glacier, Delbridge Islands and McMurdo Sound. Nearby are remnants of provisions and equipment left in 1908. Boxes of maize, dog kennels, a wheel from the Arrol-Johnston car, pony feed boxes, a snatch block from *Nimrod*, all add to the uncanny historic atmosphere pervading the area.

Inside, dominating one end of the hut, is the cooking range with a large iron pot recognisable in photographs of the time. Hams hang on a wall. And galley shelves are stacked with an assortment of Edwardian provisions. There are tinned meats and vegetables, and bottles of raspberries, gooseberries and red currants still wrapped in straw. A frame for a portable canvas bath, the Drummond acetylene lighting plant and a pony harness can be seen, along with iron beds from the Terra Nova expedition.

An inscription, "Wild and Joyce, painters, book binders etc. Gentlemen only" indicates the 'Rogue's Retreat' where the *Aurora Australis*, the first book to be printed in Antarctica, was produced in the winter of 1908. Graffiti such as "Joyce's Skinning Academy, Free!" date from the Ross Sea Party occupancy in 1916. The roulette wheel and paper for the printing press have vanished.

CAPE EVANS, ROSS ISLAND

Building, Cape Evans

Terra Nova expedition and Ross Sea Party

Beneath the slopes of brooding Mt Erebus, 13km south of Cape Royds, is Cape Evans, a headland found by the Discovery expedition and originally named the Skuary because of the many skuas to be found there. On the Terra Nova expedition Scott renamed it for his second in command, Lieutenant Edward Evans RN (later Admiral Lord Mountevans).

Departing from Port Chalmers on 29 November 1910, *Terra Nova* arrived off Cape Crozier in early January to find it unsuitable for winter quarters and after steaming into McMurdo Sound, Scott chose Cape Evans as the site for his shore station.

"I went ashore with Captain Scott to select a site for the hut," said Terra Nova carpenter, Frank Davies RN. "The surface was like cinders, quite loose, but a few inches below it was frozen solid. This formed a good foundation."

The large quantity of stores and equipment taken to Antarctica included 33 dogs, 2 Siberian and 17 Manchurian ponies, three Wolseley motor tractors and three prefabricated wooden buildings. One was destined for the 25-man shore party , another was for the Northern Party at Cape Adare and the third, intended as a scientific station at Granite Harbour, was never used. It was later acquired by Scott's agent Joseph Kinsey (later Sir Joseph) and erected on his property at Clifton, in Christchurch, New Zealand, where it remains to this day.

Davies attaching insulating material to the building at Cape Evans in 1911.—Canterbury Museum

By 17 January 1911 winter quarters were complete and the party moved in. "The word 'hut' is misleading," said Scott. "Our residence is really a house of considerable size, in every respect the finest that has been erected in the polar regions." It was nevertheless cramped accommodation for 25 men, 14.6 m long, well short of a cricket pitch in length, and 7.40m wide. The central ridge was 4.30m above the floor.

This was the base from which Scott, Edward Wilson, Lieutenant Henry Bowers RIM, Lawrence Oates and Edgar Evans (and the support parties) set out on their journey over the Ross Ice Shelf, up the massive Beardmore Glacier and across the Polar Plateau to the South Pole, arriving on 18 January 1912 to find, to their great disappointment, that Roald Amundsen had hoisted the Norwegian flag a month earlier.

A bulkhead of bottled supplies partitioned the hut into two areas, one for the 16 officers and scientists, and the other for the nine 'men' including the sailors. Three double glazed windows, oil lamps, a weekly ration of candles and two acetylene generators provided light. In winter, about 7kg of carbide kept 12 lights going throughout the day.

The floor, walls and roof were insulated with dried shredded seaweed sewn into jute quilting and Ruberoid (felt impregnated with bitumen) sealed the roof. Olive green linoleum covered the floor upon which a broad strip of coconut matting ran the length of the building. The building was sparsely heated by modern standards. The cooking stove heated the 'mess deck' and serviced a 227 litre (50 gallon) ice-fed water tank. A smaller schoolroom stove heated the 'wardroom'.

Davies salvaged some timber from the ship, and with offcuts of matchboarding and scraps of Ruberoid built stables for the ponies along the seaward side of the hut. The outer wall comprised 5.4kg (12 lb) blocks of compressed coal and 50.8kg (112 lb) bales of pony fodder. A small stove, the work of Edward Atkinson, surgeon, and Chief Engineer William Williams

RN, was installed at one end of the stables. It was fueled by seal blubber and was used to melt snow, make pemmican for the dogs and cook pony mash, as well as providing some warmth to the animals and men.

Latrines, also partitioned for officers and men, were placed between the main building and the sea and were emptied twice daily into a tide crack.

Important science including magnetic, auroral observations and meteorological observations was undertaken by Charles Wright, physicist and George Simpson, meteorologist. A magnetic observatory was erected some 75m from the south side of the main building The small timber framed shelter was clad in asbestos sheets to prevent any interference of the magnetic observations and was warmed by a small heating stove of non ferrous metal. The original shelter is intact and has since been protected by a plywood cladding. Gravity measurements were undertaken by Wright in a small cave dug from ice in the lee of a hill, soon to be known as Wind Vane Hill, near the magnetic hut. This did not provide the stable environment hoped for and observations were later carried out in Herbert Ponting's darkroom.

The ice has largely gone but the collapsed wooden structure of the cave remains. Mutton carcasses, the gift of New Zealand farmers, were stored in another cave nearby, but were inedible. Other structures included a 'garage' for motor engineer Bernard Day's motor tractors and a rock-walled hut built by Apsley Cherry-Garrard for seal skinning. He was the Assistant Zoologist.

Davies, when he returned on *Terra Nova* the following summer, built more satisfactory wooden stables to house the seven Indian mules which went south on the ship. A 28 m^2 stores annex was also added at the west end of the main building with the stables on the seaward side.

When the ship returned on its third and final trip to collect the expedition enough stores and equipment to last a twelve man party for at least a year were left at Cape Evans.

Two years later the hut became home for another expedition. The Ross Sea Party, under Captain Aeneas Mackintosh were to support Shackleton's attempt at the first crossing of the continent. Their primary task was to lay depots to the end of Minna Bluff, then at each degree of latitude south as far as Mount Hope at the foot of the Beardmore Glacier.

"On arrival our first impressions were the very decided state of neatness....little compact heaps of store cases surrounded the hut itself - sledges, snow houses, huts, electrical wire like cast off spiders web, seemed to litter the place," said Captain Mackintosh on coming ashore from *Aurora* on 16 January 1915.

Inside, they found the bunks and recesses filled with discarded clothing. They took a rough inventory and discovered much that would be of use to them, including a sledge load of old ski boots which were especially welcome as *Aurora* had sailed without any. They also located a sounding tube containing the previous party's records.

The motor tractor engineer, Aubrey Ninnis, collected many souvenirs. There was one of Captain Oates' pipes, Atkinson's tobacco pouch, Scott's whistle and boots marked RFS (Robert Falcon Scott).

Unable to find an anchorage further south at Glacier Tongue, *Aurora* returned to Cape Evans on 14 March and was moored, bow seaward, about 40m off-shore. Two anchors were buried in the beach with another two off the bow. It was thought that the ship would be safely frozen in like *Discovery* at Hut Point 13 years previously, and would provide accommodation for the 28 men. Scott's 'wardroom' heating stove was taken aboard *Aurora* and modified to burn blubber by Chief Engineer Alfred Larkman. It was then returned to the hut. An oil stove was installed in Ponting's darkroom for the Reverend Arnold Spencer-Smith.

Winter blizzards increased in intensity and on 6 May *Aurora* was blown from its moorings leaving 10 men marooned at Cape Evans with inadequate clothing and fuel. They thought the ship

Unloading supplies onto the beach at Cape Evans in 1911. R.F.Scott stands at porch.—Canterbury Museum

had gone down with all hands, but over the next ten months, *Aurora* drifted 1900km, eventually reaching Port Chalmers in New Zealand.

In preparation for depot laying, three Scott expedition Primus stoves were overhauled, while Wild and Joyce used old tents and caribou skin sleeping bags to make extra trousers, jackets and boots. In September the Girling motor tractor, which had broken down in early autumn was dragged on a sledge over sea-ice from Hut Point to Cape Evans where part of the outer stable wall was removed to provide a workshop and garage. However, after deciding not to use the tractor in the coming summer, it was pushed outside, where it remained for the next 42 years.

Later in the expedition 2400 Adélie penguin eggs were collected from Cape Royds and supplies of seal blubber were stacked in the annex.

Tragedy struck the 10 men when Spencer-Smith succumbed to scurvy and two months later Mackintosh and Hayward disappeared while traversing sea ice between Hut Point and Cape Evans.

A cross in their memory was erected on Wind Vane Hill, near the Cape Evans hut, by the survivors. A cross inscribed "A Brave Man" was also placed on Spencer-Smith's grave on the Ross Ice Shelf, by his cousin Irvine Gaze, in December 1916. This would have been covered by drifting snow and has not been seen since.

On 10 January 1917, Richards sighted *Aurora* just a few kilometres away at the ice edge.

To Captain John Davis the seven survivors, "looked very unkempt and dishevelled and smelt strongly of seal blubber." Later he recounted, "their speech was jerky, semi-hysterical and at times almost unintelligible. Their eyes had a strained and harassed look."

The rescue of the seven men stranded at Cape Evans for over two years closed the 'heroic-era' of Antarctic exploration.

Americans from the US icebreaker *Burton Island*, visited Cape Evans on 20 February 1947 during 'Operation High Jump' and again the following summer on 'Operation Windmill'. Then came the International Geophysical Year (IGY) and the Commonwealth Trans Antarctic Expedition (TAE) bringing visitors to Cape Evans in the mid-1950s. John Fletcher, a US Navy photographer, found on the wardroom table the remains of a meal started by Shackleton, Joyce, Ernest Wild and meteorologist Keith Jack just before their departure aboard *Aurora* in January 1917. The rest of the building was almost completely filled with ice.

The establishment of American and New Zealand bases on Ross Island led to renewed interest in the historic sites. Crew members of HMNZS *Endeavour* and staff from Scott Base, undertook some work, including the burning of 'rubbish', clearing snow from within the building, refelting parts of the roof, and generally tidying the environs. A dart board removed from Cape Royds by Joyce, was sent to the Dominion Museum, Wellington together with the Ross Sea Party's tractor. They are now in the Canterbury Museum, Christchurch. Forrester Davidson, Scott Base summer meteorologist during IGY visited Cape Evans in January 1958 and retrieved a pair of socks labelled Cherry-Garrard from a line in the galley. After washing them he returned them to their owner.

Quartermain and his party began work at Cape Evans, in the summer of 1960-61. The task was formidable. Only the galley remained relatively ice free, yet even here, half a metre of clear ice covered the floor firmly imprisoning the mess deck table and chairs from the Terra Nova expedition as well as the only tent landed from *Aurora*. Shelves of provisions had collapsed under the weight of snow.

Quartermain sought advice from specialists in the northern hemisphere. The only practical way to clear the building was by pick and shovel. As artefacts were located, the blocks of ice encasing them were placed outside to thaw in the twenty-four hour sunlight. Artefacts found included a bagatelle board complete with cue and balls, published scientific reports from the *Discovery*, a draft inscription by Jack for the Wind Vane Hill memorial cross, geographer Griffith Taylor's bicycle and a diary kept by Richards in 1915.

It was inevitable that some glass artefacts in the laboratory and galley would be damaged, and unfortunately no plan was made of the location of any material. Most items found were black with soot from the burning of seal blubber fuel by the Ross Sea Party.

The 'hut caretaker' programme, with New Zealand Antarctic Society volunteers, ensured on-going maintenance and during the 1970s many interesting discoveries were made. A poignant item located by Richard McElrea and Harry Burson in 'rubbish' outside the entrance was the combination man-dog sledge hauling harness used by the Ross Sea Party. Also found were fittings for Scott's motor tractors and Oates' long johns, once Spencer-Smith's souvenir.

In July 1985 the HSMC recommended the removal of selected artefacts from the Ross Island and Cape Adare sites. Criteria included uniqueness, historical importance, and the need for conservation to ensure survival. The next year a collection of important items was taken from Cape Evans, Cape Royds and Hut Point, for conservation in New Zealand. Cape Adare artefacts were uplifted in 1990.

With the founding of the Antarctic Heritage Trust in 1987, a start was made in 1988-89 to attach a Butylclad rubber covering to plywood screwed on the roof cladding to make the building snow proof. This task was completed by the Trust's team led by John Newton in 1991.

The extent of conservation to be undertaken at Cape Evans is immense and the associated problems have long been recognised. In 1970 New Zealand Antarctic Society 'caretakers' Charles Satterthwaite and Stan Smith, drew attention to rusting bed wires and the dessication and shrinkage of building timber.

Loading the Ross Sea Party tractor on to HMNZS Endeavour *in 1957—Forrester Davidson*

Similar problems have been highlighted by Harrowfield and Chris Buckley in 1977-78, by professional conservator Jack Fry in 1981-82 and more recently Lynn Campbell.

Conservators have determined that the extreme dry conditions characteristic of the Antarctic environment, are not always present within the historic buildings. It is not the "warm, dry, Cape Evans home" described by Scott in 1911, but cold and damp. Only by obtaining detailed records of temperature and relative humidity fluctuations will it be possible to accurately gauge such effects as visitor presence on the internal climate and perhaps relate this to the degeneration of artefacts. The question of high ultra-violet light levels has to be addressed and appropriate steps taken, possibly by fitting filters to windows.

The Trust has undertaken archaeological excavation around the Cape Evans building, including the 1911 stores annex and stables, by a team comprising Ritchie, Nelson Cross and Fyfe. This work has been made easier since 1988 by the use of a small handheld percussion tool to fracture ice around buried or semi-buried artefacts.

Discoveries of artefacts have provided new insight into the early expeditions and as historical archaeologist Ivor Noel Hume says, "It is imperative that we realise that the techniques of archaeology can be usefully applied to any period, no matter how recent, if by digging something up we can learn more than is to be found in written records."

There is still much to be done at this historic site. The environs need resurveying to provide a detailed map pin-pointing artefact positions, and consideration given to the protection of some of them. There is scope for recording artefacts on the sea-bed including the motor tractor lost in 1911.

An important part of the Trust's work con-

The galley at Cape Evans, 1960-61, with chairs last used by the Ross Sea Party, embedded in ice.
—J.M.Sandman

cerns site interpretation and display to assist visitors in understanding the history associated with Cape Evans. The Trust believes that any display should create minimal intrusion.

The Cape Evans building contains many artefacts linking four year's occupation by two expeditions. There are quantities of provisions, books, items of clothing, improvised boots (some soled), scientific equipment, early morse keys and even an emperor penguin skin stuffed in 1916.

Empty provision cases nailed to walls once held diaries and other personal effects. Magazine cut-outs on a wall include the back view of a woman showering - but obscured from the waist down by running water. Dominating the central space is the wardroom table, and in the annex can be seen Griffith Taylor's bicycle, a cache of seal blubber and a box of penguin eggs collected in 1916. In the stables the stencilled names of the seven mules are recorded now, for posterity.

Outside are many items of interest. The magnetic hut, the site of the two ice caves, Apsley Cherry-Garrard's stone shelter, rolls of aluminium telephone wire, cases of petrol for the motor tractors, the meteorological screen and the pony tethering wire from Scott's expedition. Links with the Ross Sea Party include seal and dog skeletons, Aurora's two anchors and prominent on Wind Vane Hill, the memorial cross.

American biologists have found the sea floor adjacent to Cape Evans, littered with historic artefacts. Trygve Gran recorded on 18 August 1912, "We cleaned up our cubicle (occupied by Taylor, Debenham and Gran) this morning. We dumped Griffith Taylor's bed and a couple of tons of rubbish into the Ross Sea." A leather ski boot in perfect condition has been recovered and is now in the Canterbury Museum.

"Cape Evans is a very evocative place," says Australian archaeologist Michael Pearson, "probably because of the wealth of artefacts which remain and the plethora of images created by the published documents and photographs by Ponting. The hut to me was still Scott's, and while the presence of the Ross Sea Party was clear, when you looked closely, it did not overshadow the stronger presence of Scott."

Cross, Wind Vane Hill, Cape Evans
Ross Sea Party

Wind Vane Hill is a small rise just northeast of the extremity of Cape Evans. The name dates from the Terra Nova expedition. It was the site of an anemometer (and other instruments) connected by overhead wires to recording instruments in the winter quarters.

Although the Ross Sea Party's depot laying task in 1916 was fully accomplished, it was not without tragic cost. During the trek to the final depot at 83° 30'S near Mt Hope at the foot of the Beardmore Glacier, Spencer-Smith, along with his five companions, contracted scurvy. The depot was laid on 26 January and the party turned for home 560km away, soon carrying Spencer-Smith who was now too weak to walk. For five days the party was beset by a howling blizzard, their food ran out and although Richards, Joyce and Hayward were able to reach the next cache about 20km away, and bring back fresh supplies, Spencer-Smith, whose physical condition had rapidly deteriorated, died within a few kilometres of Hut Point on 9 March 1916.

Mackintosh, who had to be carried in, Hayward, Richards, Joyce and Wild, although all scurvy-stricken, eventually reached Hut Point nine days later where they recuperated on a diet of fresh seal meat. After seven weeks of forced inactivity Mackintosh and Hayward decided they were fit enough to make for Cape Evans. Leaving Hut Point on 8 May, the pair set out across the dangerously thin sea ice only

The cross on Wind Vane Hill erected in memory of Mackintosh, Spencer-Smith and Hayward who died in 1916.—Colin Monteath / Hedgehog House New Zealand

to be engulfed by a severe southerly blizzard - they were never seen again.

Before departing on *Aurora*, one final sad duty remained for the rescued survivors. On 16 January 1917, Jack and Wild erected a cross to the memory of their three companions attached to which was a copper cylinder containing a message written by Shackleton. This was removed in 1947 to the National Maritime Museum, Greenwich, England. The draft of the intended inscription for the cross, discovered when the Cape Evans building was being cleared of ice, is now in the Canterbury Museum. In 1961 Quartermain showed it to Keith Jack then living in retirement in Australia who said the intention was to carve it on the cross but there had been insufficient time. It was eventually engraved on a Formica plaque placed at the base of the cross and unveiled on 9 November 1963, by Sir Bernard Ferguson, Governor-General of New Zealand.

The cross, although weathered, is in sound condition with the original metal mounting for the message cylinder still attached.

CAPE CROZIER, ROSS ISLAND

Message Post, Cape Crozier

Discovery expedition

After considering Wood Bay and Granite Harbour as wintering places, *Discovery* proceeded east to Cape Crozier on Ross Island where a message post for the relief ship, *Morning*, was erected on 22 January 1902. A metal cylinder containing an account of the expedition's movements to date was attached. *Discovery* then proceeded to explore 'The Barrier', and unable to find a suitable place for wintering, returned to Ross Island.

The message post at Cape Crozier when erected in the Adélie penguin rookery, 1902—R.F.Scott

The message post at Cape Crozier, 1976.Showing Scott Base dog handler Gary Bowcock.—Colin Monteath / Hedgehog House New Zealand

With the ship safely moored at Winter Quarters Bay, a party set out for Cape Crozier on 4 March to up-date the record. Travel through soft snow resulted in the trip being aborted and it was on the return journey that George Vince lost his life in early autumn. In late September-early October another visit was made when emperor penguin eggs were collected and a new tin was attached advising the relief ship of the expedition's whereabouts. Two subsequent trips were made to examine the emperor penguin rookery.

The message post has since been visited by several parties and although weathered, it still stands. In July 1985 Robert Swan of the Footsteps of Scott Expedition described the post as "A forlorn and pathetic marker, a hurriedly erected joist, leaning from the vertical in a cairn of boulders, its grain blasted into high relief by countless storms. The record cylinder has long gone."

"Cape Crozier is a strange, enchanted place," he says. "Its topography is of an intimate human scale, distinct from the callous vastness of the Barrier and the rarefied grandeur of Mount Terror, under which it nestles."

Rock Hut, Cape Crozier
Terra Nova expedition

Cape Crozier, the eastern extremity of Ross Island was named by Ross in 1841 after Commander Francis Crozier RN, Captain of HMS *Terror*.

The first recorded visit to Cape Crozier, was made in October 1902 by a sledging party from the Discovery expedition led by Lieutenant Charles Royds RN. They discovered an emperor penguin rookery now known to be the southernmost in the world.

Terra Nova expedition chief scientist Edward Wilson hoped to establish a link between reptiles and birds and wanted to visit Cape Crozier to observe the emperor penguin's unique winter breeding cycle. In the polar darkness of late June 1911, Wilson, together with Bowers and Cherry-Garrard, set out on a journey lasting 36 days.

They arrived at the Cape on 14 July and the small party built a 3.6 x 2.4m rock-walled hut faced with snow slabs, on an exposed spur.

"The weather wall was a foot higher than the lee," wrote Wilson, "and the entrance, in the lee wall, just allowed us to crawl in on all fours.

They laid a sledge across the walls to support the strong canvas roof which had earlier been prepared with a long valance to weigh down all round.

The party experienced a severe blizzard with temperatures of -77°F (-60°C). This unroofed the hut and their perilous position was alleviated by the fortuitous recovery of their tent. Leaving a sledge and other equipment they made a desperate dash for Cape Evans which was reached early in August. The journey was later termed 'The Worst Journey in the World'.

Forty-six years later, in March 1957, Sir Edmund Hillary and his party from the Commonwealth Trans Antarctic Expedition travelled to Cape Crozier while testing Ferguson farm tractors for depot laying. They came across an old pemmican tin and decided to make a concerted effort to locate the historic site. En-

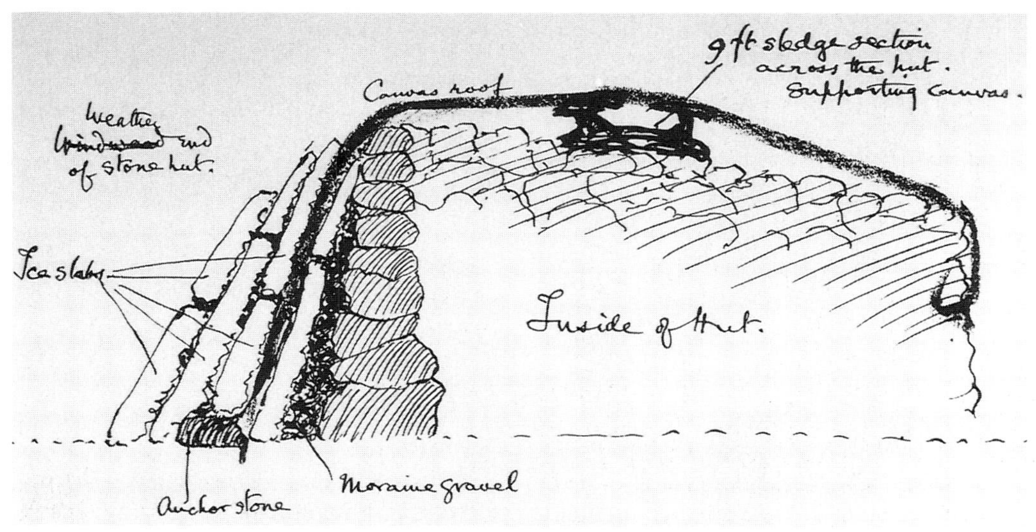

Drawing of Crozier rock hut from Wilson's diary of the Terra Nova expedition

Remains of the rock hut at Cape Crozier in December 1993. Mount Terror in background.—NZAP

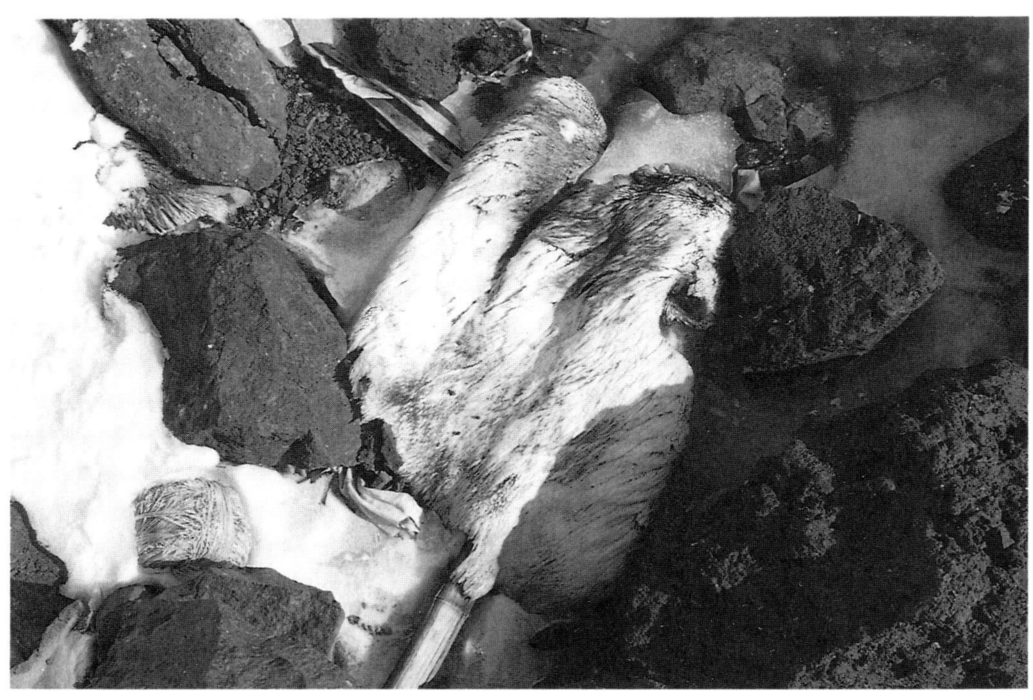

Emperor penguin skins in the remains of the Cape Crozier rock hut.—Roger Fyfe

gineer, Murray Ellis, who had with him a copy of Cherry-Garrard's classic *Worst Journey in the World*, later wrote, "After tea and after consulting book again as to position of old hut, Ed had a notion it was on a ridge not far from where we were."

The hut, (merely four stone walls) was located by Hillary on a spur leading off Mt Terror about 500m further down the ridge that the party was on.

"The old nine foot sledge was iced in as was an old pick axe," said Ellis. "We dug the sledge out but could find no note which was mentioned in book. Finally returned to camp in semi-darkness about 9.30 pm bringing sledge, axe and some bamboo poles."

Ellis and radio operator Chief Petty Officer Peter Mulgrew RNZN, again visited the site and recovered scientific gear which had been left in one corner under some pieces of penguin. There was also a box containing pemmican, cheese and two tins of salt, and a larger box with test tubes, bottles of alcohol, alum, several pencils (for Wilson's sketching no doubt), envelopes with Terra Nova's stamp on them and a storm lantern.

They returned to camp with as much of the gear as possible and left behind a blubber stove and an old hurricane lamp.

Nearly a hundred artefacts (listed on p.96 in Sir Edmund's book, *No Latitude for Error*) were returned to New Zealand and distributed among various museums. The sledge and German Bat brand hurricane lantern are presently in the Canterbury Museum.

Since then, several visits have been made to this historic site. In January 1959 surveyor Bruce Alexander of the New Zealand Geological and Survey Expedition reported, "The emperor penguin skins collected by Wilson's party, some of his collecting bottles, bamboo poles, remnants of the canvas roof and other items are still there. It is hoped they will remain there permanently."

Antarctic Treaty plaques were placed on the windswept spur by Scott Base staff during the autumn of 1977.

In mid-winter, 1985, during the Footsteps of Scott Expedition, leader Robert Swan, Dr Michael Stroud and Gareth Wood retraced the famous journey man-hauling sledges to Cape Crozier. After arriving in early July, with the temperature at -41°C. Swan wrote, "The igloo is a barren inhospitable pile of stones. Fragments of the green Willesden canvas are still there, weighed under rocks placed around the remains of the rough walls. Within its cramped confines, other historic debris abounds: the thick feathered pelt of an emperor penguin, killed in all probability to provide fuel for the blubber stove; the battered and rusted shell of a small lantern; a woollen sock, perhaps one of those used to stop a draught in the leaking walls; and a sledging box, its thin wood bleached to the colour of bone, blocked full of blue ice in which were set rusting tins of food."

On 27 November 1990, Garth Varcoe found that there was not a great deal of the 'igloo' left except for rocks, a ball of string, bamboo poles, shredded canvas, emperor skins, a scarf, wire and a box. More recently, Fyfe, inspecting the site for the Trust, found all objects in an advanced state of decay, and noted that some of the artefacts appear to be the result of later placement. When visited in January 1992, more than 100mm of water topped with ice was in the interior. Fyfe says there is little purpose in undertaking an excavation at this stage as the majority of artefacts are already visible and if excavated there is no safe reserve storage. The Trust has yet to decide what work needs to be done on this site. Meanwhile,

"These are the fragments of canvas green
That round Cape Crozier can still be seen."

MOUNT CIS, ROSS ISLAND
Supply Depot and Camp Site,
Mount Cis, near Cape Barne
Terra Nova expedition

One of the rocky outcrops which extend down from Fang Ridge on Mt Erebus is a small volcanic cone approximately 190m high. It is named Mt Cis after one of the Nimrod expedition's dogs.

On 2 December 1912, after the Northern Party had recuperated for two weeks at Cape Evans, geologist Raymond Priestley led a team comprised of Dickason, Abbott, a second geologist Frank Debenham and steward Frederick Hooper to the summit of Mount Erebus to survey the old crater. Camp was made six days later and while Debenham and Dickason were left to complete the survey the others achieved the second ascent of Erebus before returning to Cape Royds on the 15th. Hooper wrote " Had lunch at 1700 feet and carried on down to a large cone where we depot(ed) one tent and cooker and a few tins of biscuits for Mr P & D for their plane-tabling work which they are going to do at Cape Royds till the ship arrives." (P & D refers to Priestley and Debenham)

Sixty five years later, in December 1977, when a New Zealand survey party was inland from Cape Barne, Nigel Nalder observed through his theodolite, the profile of a pick on the skyline above a rock outcrop. Nalder and field assistant Russell Brice investigated and discovered not only a well weathered pick of the same type as found at Cape Evans, but nearby, tins, bottles and rope fragments indicating a possible camp site. The tins, although corroded, were in reasonable condition.

It is presumed that the site, which has not been examined since 1977, is the one described by Hooper.

OBSERVATION HILL, ROSS ISLAND

Cross, Observation Hill

Terra Nova expedition

Observation Hill is a 230m high volcanic cone surmounting Cape Armitage at the southern end of Hut Point Peninsula on Ross Island. From the days of the Discovery expedition it has provided an excellent lookout point in all directions.

It is the site of the most famous of several memorial crosses erected in the Ross Sea area.

The supply depot site at Mount Cis on the slopes of Mount Erebus.—Nigel Nalder

The cross on Observation Hill after the June 1993 storm.—Ed Anderson

At the close of the Terra Nova expedition, carpenter Frank Davies, spent 30 hours making a cross in excess of 3.6m in length and 1.8m across of Australian jarrah in memory of Scott, Wilson, Bowers, Oates, and Petty Officer Edgar Evans who perished returning from the South Pole in March 1912. It bears an inscription, selected by Cherry-Garrard from Tennyson's *Ulysses*, "To strive, to seek, to find, and not to yield".

But this was not the first monument erected in Antarctica to the memory of Scott's party. A cross made from Gran's skis, was placed on the large snow cairn built over the tent that entombed the bodies of Scott, Bowers and Wilson.

Early in the morning of 20 January 1913 Atkinson, leader of the southern search party that had found Scott's final camp, led a group ashore to erect the cross on Observation Hill. It was made in two halves and took 8 hours to haul on two sledges across the sea-ice from the ship to Hut Point. From there it had to be manhandled to the summit of Observation Hill.

"About 11 am we took the remaining portions of the cross to the top of the hill," said Davies. "It is a very steep climb. I had the various parts all ready for bolting together and we had it erected in three hours."

After giving three cheers for their departed comrades, photographs were taken and the sad party returned to *Terra Nova* which sailed for New Zealand the next day.

On at least two occasions the 130kg cross has been blown over. When re-erected in September 1974 the orientation was changed with the inscription facing north. The last time the cross was blown over was during a storm in June 1993.

It was removed to Scott Base for repairs before being returned to it's site with a new concrete base. It was rededicated in January 1994 when 120 New Zealanders and Americans, in teams of 15, carried it to the summit of Observation Hill. This mode of transport was felt to be more appropriate than using a helicopter, a sentiment based out of respect for the men who originally hand-carried it up the steep hill.

Unfortunately, the memorial has been subjected to vandalism. Bronze bolts holding the components of the cross together have been removed, visitors have scratched their names into the wood and screws have been taken from the four language Antarctic Treaty plaques. The cross, although weathered, still has traces of the original paint, but the inscription, now correctly facing south, is deteriorating.

FERRAR GLACIER, SOUTH VICTORIA LAND

Supply Depot, Ferrar Glacier

Discovery expedition

The Ferrar Glacier named after Hartley Ferrar a geologist on the Discovery expedition, is about 56km long and flows from the Polar Plateau west of the Royal Society Range to New Harbour in McMurdo Sound.

On 26 October 1903 Scott placed a depot near the outlet of the Ferrar Glacier before sledging up it to the Polar Plateau.

During Scott's last expedition, the second Western Party, while skirting New Harbour on 10 February 1912 came across a Spratt's biscuit box which was evidently left by the 1902 expedition.

The remains of the depot were located by Hillary, Ellis and Jim Bates while testing their tractors in September 1957. The depot has not been seen since.

Supply Depot, Cathedral Rocks, Ferrar Glacier

Terra Nova expedition

The Cathedral Rocks were discovered and named on 7 December 1902 by Lieutenant

The re-erected cross on Observation Hill, January 1994. In the foreground are Grant Avery, Scott Base Science Technician (left) and Dave Lucas, Engineering Services Manager.—NZAP (Yvonne Martin)

View of the Ferrar Glacier, westward from New Harbour.—NZAP (Garth Varcoe)

Albert Armitage RNR, leader of a Discovery expedition sledging party. The name is descriptive of the feature which consists of a series of abrupt cliffs cut by short glaciers and surmounted by sharp peaks. It extends for about 12km along the south side of the Ferrar Glacier and forms part of the north shoulder of the Royal Society Range.

On 28 January 1911 Griffith Taylor, when leading the first western party, climbed above the Ferrar Glacier and saw to the south-west the three giant gables of Cathedral Rocks.

Two days later, they camped on a near-by glacial moraine, and in accordance with Scott's instructions, placed a depot. The next morning two week's provisions were taken and a note tied to the depot flag indicating their anticipated return. An emperor penguin killed for fresh meat was left at the site.

The party returned after 10 days to find the

Cathedral Rocks on the south side of the Ferrar Glacier.—NZAP (Robert Findlay)

food uncovered, the pemmican and butter melted by the sun and the emperor devoured by skuas. They then continued mapping down the Ferrar to Butter Point. The depot has not been seen since.

DAVIS BAY, SOUTH VICTORIA LAND

Supply Depot, Davis Bay (now Salmon Bay)

Terra Nova eexpedition

Davis Bay is a small bay north of Cape Chocolate on the south coast of Victoria Land. Davis Stream flows into the bay from the Davis Glacier. All three were named in February 1911 by the second western party to honour the eminent American geomorphologist, Professor William Morris Davis.

When studying the geology of the area, Taylor's party placed a depot on glacial moraine at Cape Chocolate. It has not been established whether the party returned to the depot after completing their examination of the Koettlitz Glacier. The depot has not been visited since.

GRANITE HARBOUR, SOUTH VICTORIA LAND

Granite House, Cape Geology, Granite Harbour

Terra Nova expedition

Cape Geology, a low gravel-covered point marks the western limit of Botany Bay in Granite Harbour, Victoria Land. It was charted and named by the second western party of the Terra Nova expedition, "in memory of the chief object of our journey."

Granite Harbour, discovered by the earlier Discovery expedition while searching for winter quarters in January 1902, gained its name from the many large granite boulders found along the shoreline.

Having exhausted their kerosene and to protect their tent, the Terra Nova expedition's sec-

Terraces and mouth of the Davis Stream from Cape Chocolate December 1958.—NZAP

The rock hut at Cape Geology in 1911.—Trygve Gran

ond western party of Taylor, Gran, Debenham and Petty Officer Robert Forde RN, built 'Granite House' at Cape Geology in early December 1911. This rough shelter was used primarily as a kitchen with cooking done on a sheet-iron blubber stove brought from Cape Evans. Measuring 2.75m square and 1.57m high, it was enclosed on three sides by large granite boulders with a sledge forming a roof-tree over which fresh seal skins were stretched and anchored down with heavy rocks. A flue was added to the stove and the finished shelter was named after a building in a Jules Verne novel. Moss was stuffed in wall cracks to keep out draughts.

"The stove smokes badly," wrote Taylor, " but gives off enormous flames and heat."

Soon soot and oil filled the bottom of the stove and ran out over the rocks covering the snowy floor. " We had to stand in this fearful mixture, which is dirtier than the grease in a foul motor engine, and much more ubiquitous," said Taylor. In an endeavour to clean up the mess, Forde spread gravel over the floor.

On 4 December they made ready for the next stage of their trip, with Forde preparing seal steaks for the journey and Taylor writing a note

Remains of the rock shelter, Cape Geology 1992. —NZAP (Rod Seppelt)

The sledge at Cape Geology 23 November 1959.—Bill Meserve

to Captain Harry Pennell telling him they were going inland until 8 January. They returned to Granite House next day to find it half filled with snow.

The party was off again on 14 December exploring the western coast of Granite Harbour. After working at Cape Cuff, they moved on to the next cape which closely resembled a skyscraper and which they called Flatiron. They then continued on to a feature they named Devil's Punchbowl. Returning to Cape Geology, the four explorers spent Christmas Day relaxing at the rock shelter.

After using 'Granite House' as their base for the previous six weeks, on 13 January 1912, Griffith Taylor decided to break camp and set out for Cape Roberts. "Forde and I packed everything which we should need for sledging at Evans Cove on a good sledge," he wrote. " We packed the specimens and some articles not now necessary on the `roof-tree' sledge. This necessitated dismantling Granite Hut and very woe-begone it looked, with the seal skins flapping dismally on its walls."

At the close of the Terra Nova expedition the ship called at Cape Geology on 23 January and retrieved 300kg of rocks and fossils.

Granite House was next visited by American geologists of the Tufts College National Science Foundation Antarctic Expedition on 23 November 1959. Numerous artefacts including a 3.75m sledge with an ice axe standing next to it, were listed by Bill Meserve. Two books, Verne's *The Secret of the Island*, the last volume of the trilogy *L'Ile Mysterieuse* published in 1875, and Edgar Allan Poe's *Tales of Mystery and Imagination*, both in perfect condition, were found lying on the sledge. They were taken back to the United States where their condition created much interest amongst paper conservators, before being returned to their owners, Taylor and Debenham.

Ray Logie, a member of a New Zealand scientific party in October 1962, noted "the old stone hut standing well, seal skin roof has fallen in, seal skins are still attached to ropes and room has skins on each wall. Below the camp site there is a man-hauling sledge, old fuel cans, old boots and small piece of canvas, also an ice-axe which will be taken back to Scott Base."

On 19 December 1981, New Zealanders

The sledge at Cape Geology 16 December 1993.—ICAIR (Colin Harris)

Gerry Turner and Jack Fry with US scientist Ursula Marvin found Granite House still in good condition but the sledge had already begun to disintegrate. Malcolm Macfarlane and Pat Nolan from Scott Base in November 1990 reported that the deterioration was accelerating.

A tobacco tin containing the note written by Taylor during the 1911-12 summer to Captain Pennell of *Terra Nova* was found between two rocks about 8m from Granite House is now in the Scott Polar Research Institute, University of Cambridge, England. It reads:

> 14-1-12
>
> Dear Pennell,
> We have left these
> headquarters (Camp Geology) for a
> more accessible one on Cape Roberts
> which is on the route any ship or
> party must take to reach the
> Rendezvous.
> We shall wait at C Roberts
> (8 m east of this) until Jan 31
> then push overland (via the
> Piedmont to C Bernacchi
> & Hut Point
> Fuller details on the
> Signal Flag 500 feet up the
> Rendezvous Bluff & 1 mile east
> of this.
>
> Griffith Taylor

Expedition members reported Granite House to be still intact, with some of the moss still between the blocks. One seal skin was on the floor inside, one over the north-eastern wall and a third on the ground nearby. In addition to the sledge, pieces of calico, fragments of paper and rusted tins, including a complete paraffin tin, were on the floor. A similar tin was nearby. The sledge has totally disintegrated.

The camp site at the Devil's Punchbowl, Granite Harbour, December 1911.—Griffith Taylor

Camp Site, Devils Punchbowl, GraniteHarbour
Terra Nova expedition

The Devil's Punchbowl is a bowl-shaped cove (an empty cirque drowned by the sea) in the south west corner of Granite Harbour between Devil's Ridge and the south side of the Flatiron.

For three days from 20 December 1911, the second western party camped at Devil's Punchbowl to enable Griffith Taylor and Frank Debenham to complete mapping the area before returning to Cape Geology for Christmas.

The camp site has not been found since.

CAPE ROBERTS, SOUTH VICTORIA LAND

Supply Depot, and Cairn Cape Roberts

Terra Nova expedition

Cape Roberts, at the southern entrance to Granite Harbour was discovered by the Nimrod expedition's Magnetic Pole party and named after William Roberts, assistant zoologist and cook on the expedition.

The second western party of the Terra Nova expedition arrived at Cape Roberts from Cape Geology in mid-January 1912 to allow Debenham to make a plane-table survey of the area, after which it was planned they would be picked up by the ship. On Scott's instructions, Griffith Taylor was to build a stone hut and provision it with seal meat in case the ship was unable to uplift them.

They waited until February when Taylor wrote a letter to Captain Pennell which, after it was signed by all, was placed in a matchbox attached to a flag pole on the highest point of the cape. The party left Cape Roberts the next day.

"I remorselessly weeded out everyone's gear," said Taylor. "We took nothing but what we stood up in and our notes and instruments. Luckily, most of Debenham's and all of Gran's negatives

The cairn and depot found by the TAE Northern Exploration Party on windswept Cape Roberts in 1957.—Richard Brooke

were films, but I had to leave nearly all my plates and cherished Browning." (Poems)

One day's march took them to Cape Bernacchi, where, in the previous November they had left a depot protected by a cairn of granite. Four days later the party made for Butter Point, where they were collected by *Terra Nova*.

The following spring, after wintering over on Inexpressible Island, the Northern Party reached Cape Roberts on 29 October finding the cache of provisions left by Taylor.

"It seemed almost too good to be true," wrote Campbell. "One and three-quarter tins of biscuits, a small bag of raisins, ditto of sugar, tea, cocoa, butter and lard. Some clothes, diaries and specimens from Granite Harbour. Dividing the provisions between the two tents we soon had a hoosh going and had such a feed of biscuit, butter and lard, we had not had for nine months followed up with thick sweet cocoa."

The next day, Campbell noted, " The change of diet has done Browning good already. I took all the food, books, specimens and records of Taylor's party leaving only the old clothes. I also left a note saying we were well."

Forty five years later, surveyor Richard Brooke and geologists Bernie Gunn and Guyon Warren with dog handler Murray Douglas of the TAE Northern Exploration Party, arrived at Cape Roberts on 15 October 1957 after three weeks sledging through wet snow. Brooke located the cairn that marked the remains of Taylor's depot and found a number of articles, including a blubber stove, a variety of very worn out socks and gloves, a thick woollen vest and a red and white Norwegian jersey. There was also a canvas bag and a film changing bag in good condition, both marked Debenham. Warren reported that the bamboo pole was still very firm and straight though pretty weather-beaten.

These items together with a mummified seal

Remains of the depot on Depot Island when located in November 1984.—Mark Mabin

carcass, were flown back to Scott Base by Flying Officer Bill Cranfield RNZAF, second pilot of the Royal New Zealand Air Force Antarctic Flight who, with Squadron Leader John Claydon RNZAF, had been resupplying the northern party by air. Debenham's changing bag, in mint condition, is on loan to Canterbury Museum from the Museum of New Zealand (previously Dominion Museum).

No reference has been found of any later visit to the depot site although in 1988-89, Alex Pyne located two sections of corroded, flattened tubing which may have been the chimney for the blubber stove taken from 'Granite House'.

DEPOT ISLAND

Supply Depot, Ross Sea

Terra Nova expedition

Depot Island is a small granitic island some three kilometres north-west of Cape Ross on the Victoria Land coast. Originally charted as a point by *Discovery*, and subsequently re-classified an island, on 21 October 1908, by Nimrod expedition's South Magnetic Pole Party, it was named because of the depot of rock specimens left there by Professor Edgeworth David.

While sledging down the coast from Inexpressible Island four years later, Campbell's northern party saw the bamboo marker from some distance off. Campbell and Priestley climbed to the top of the island and collected the rock specimens from the depot and also a tin containing four letters addressed to Mrs David, Dr Mawson, Lt. Shackleton and the Commanding Officer, *Nimrod*.

When geographer Mark Mabin called at the island on 13 November 1984, a rusted paraffin tin, bamboo and a ski pole were found. The type of fuel tin suggests this equipment was abandoned by the Northern Party. There is no record of more recent visits to Depot Island.

Looking towards the Taylor Valley with Cape Bernacchi in the foreground, 9 December 1984.—Trevor Chinn

CAPE BERNACCHI, SOUTH VICTORIA LAND

Campsite, Supply Depot and Cairn, Cape Bernacchi

Terra Nova expedition

Cape Bernacchi, is a rocky cape between Bernacchi Bay and New Harbour on the coast of Victoria Land. It was named by Scott after Louis C. Bernacchi, veteran of the 1899 Southern Cross expedition and later Discovery's physicist.

Arriving from Cape Roberts on 8 February 1912, Griffith Taylor, set up a survey camp and on the instruction of Scott, established an emergency depot with one week's provisions in case the sea ice went out.

"So we carried up a half-tin of biscuit, and filled it with butter, pemmican, and chocolate," said Taylor. After protecting the cache with a cairn of granite topped with a bamboo and flag the party broke camp and set out for Butter Point two days later.

On 1 November the Northern Party, also enroute for Butter Point, replenished their supplies from Taylor's depot. "The pemmican and raisins were most acceptable as we had finished ours," said Campbell.

Consisting of a few bamboo poles and a circle of boulders, a possible camp site was found at Cape Bernacchi by a New Zealand field party on 9 November 1987, but there was no trace of the depot which was presumably all taken by the Northern Party. There is no record of the cairn.

BUTTER POINT, SOUTH VICTORIA LAND

Supply Depot, Butter Point, Bowers Piedmont Glacier

Terra Nova expedition

Butter Point, on the north-eastern end of the Bowers Piedmont Glacier, forms the south side

The depot being placed on the Bowers Piedmont Glacier at Butter Point 1912.—J.Dennistoun. Canterbury Museum

of the entrance to New Harbour in Victoria Land. It was found, and named by Scott on the Discovery expedition. On 14 October 1902, Scott depoted one tin of butter for each of the three sledging parties. He wrote, "It was here that on our return journey we could first hope to obtain fresh seal-meat and, in preparation for this great event, a tin of butter was carried and left at this point for each party."

On 13 October 1908, Professor David, Mawson and Alistair Mackay of the Nimrod expedition, while on their way to the South Magnetic Pole, left two 12.3kg (27lb) tins of wholemeal plasmon biscuits and spare clothing at Butter Point.

When the Terra Nova expedition entered McMurdo Sound in January 1911, the first western geological party, consisting of Griffith Taylor, Debenham, Wright and Edgar Evans, deposited a cache at Butter Point.

"On the summit of a snow ridge, about half a mile away, we saw the pole of the depot left by the 1907 expedition," said Taylor. It contained a few odd pieces of clothing, tins of food and a tube of Hazelcream with David scratched on it. After souveniring these items they made their own depot at the same spot, leaving 14 cases of provisions for the next summer.

With the arrival of spring, Scott, Wilson, Bowers, George Simpson, and Edgar Evans, left further supplies for the Granite Harbour expedition who arrived at Butter Point on 17 November. In Gran's words, "We have dug out the depot - both Shackleton's old stores and those we laid down last year. They were all in cases and we spent several hours tonight breaking down the provisions into smaller bags."

After twelve weeks in the field, Griffith Taylor's party returned to Butter Point finding the depot blown over and wrecked.

The remains of the Butter Point depot, November 1986. Leo Slattery.—NZAP (Garth Varcoe)

When *Terra Nova* arrived three days later, on the second of it's three voyages to Antarctica for Scott's expedition, the ship was moored bow on to the ice and the depot replenished.

The polar party was by now presumed dead, and with concern felt for the Northern Party, Atkinson anticipated they might sledge south to McMurdo Sound. Further supplies were therefore left at Butter Point on April 20 after a dangerous trip across the sea-ice by Wright, and Petty Officers Patrick Keohane and Thomas Williamson.

The Northern Party arrived on 2 November and after their long trek down the Victoria Land coast, Priestley wrote, "Here we saw a huge stack of cases which must have contained provisions enough to keep us all going for months... Crowning all was a large bamboo with a tin lashed to it and a note from Atkinson dated April 12, 1912."

There was oatmeal, biscuits, butter, lard, sugar, chocolate, bacon, hams, jam, tea, candles, lamp-oil, and a dozen other things. After taking a few luxuries, chocolate and jam, the party crossed McMurdo Sound as fast as possible.

The final visitors to Butter Point during the 'heroic-era' were Shackleton, Joyce and Wild on 11 January 1917 searching for Mackintosh and Hayward at the close of the Aurora Relief Expedition.

The Ross Sea Party of the TAE placed a depot at Butter Point in 1957. The stores, which included butter, 200 cakes of chocolate, canned peas and Christmas hams. were discovered on 17 November 1980 by a Scott Base survey party.

The Terra Nova expedition depot remained unseen until October 1985 when Garth Varcoe, while driving across the ice to the New Zealand CIROS drilling camp at Butter Point, discovered what he first thought to be part of Sir Edmund Hillary's stores placed prior to depot laying for the journey to the South Pole. Back at the site a few weeks later, Varcoe reexamined the find. "I opened a wooden case and took some samples back to Scott Base," he said. " We realised some of the tins I'd collected were identical to containers on display at Scott's Cape Evans hut."

After digging out the top layer of cases, tins of raspberry and plum jam, three frozen rolls of bacon packed in wheat husks, egg powder, sardines, malted cocoa, sugar cubes, powdered milk, pearl barley, Liptons tea, candles, a canvas haversack with a tin of matches, and a bamboo marker pole were found. Because the site was in danger of being lost, a selection of food was taken back to Scott Base.

Varcoe said there was far more at the dump than was originally apparent. "Unfortunately it is nigh impossible to successfully recover much of this material as it has become embedded in the ice," he said. "All boxes were in reasonable condition on the outside with their metal corner edges intact.

A representative collection of the provisions, has been recovered but some, French sardines and jam, were consumed at the drilling site.

In January 1988 Neville Ritchie and Nelson Cross from Scott Base visited the site and recovered bars of chocolate, tea, a box of dates, edible candles and two boxes of butter. Officer in Charge, Graeme Ayres said, ".. part of Antarctica's history had come to life with the arrival of these artefacts at Scott Base."

Today, nothing visible remains of one of the most important 'heroic-era' field depot in the Ross Sea region.

MOUNT BETTY, QUEEN MAUD MOUNTAINS

Amundsen's Cairn, Mount Betty, Queen Maud Mountains.

Norwegian Antarctic expedition

Mount Betty (381m) is situated at the northeast extremity of the Herbert Range, Queen Maud Mountains. It was discovered in November 1911 by Roald Amundsen on his way to

'Amundsen's Cairn' when visited in 1963.—Peter Barrett

the Pole and named for Betty Andersson, his family's nurse and housekeeper. The cairn is on a small ridge overlooking the Ross Ice Shelf, on the north side of Bigend Saddle.

Amundsen left a small cache of provisions at Mt Betty on the outward journey, and when he returned on 6 January 1912, built a small rock cairn. The only depot on his entire trip, it covered the remaining 17 litres of paraffin, two boxes of matches (each containing 20 packets) as well as an account of his expedition. "Possibly someone may find a use for these things in the future," he wrote.

The cairn was inspected on 28 December 1929 by the geological party of Richard E. Byrd's 1928-30 United States Antarctic Expedition under Dr Laurence M.Gould.

"It was with almost reverent hands that we took a few rocks from the side of the cairn so that we could see what was in it without in any way disturbing the shape or structure," Gould wrote later.

"It was the climax, the high spot of the summer for all of us, when I pried off the lid of this tiny can and took out of it two little pieces of paper. One was just a piece rudely torn from a book and contained the names and addresses of Oscar Wisting and Johansen who helped Amundsen build the cairn, and the other," he said, "was a page carefully torn from the notebook of Amundsen himself. We did not need to be able to read the Norwegian to make out the fact that he had on this paper told of his successful achievement of the South Pole." (Johansen was not a member of the Pole party.)

The site has also been visited by a University of Michigan team under Dr Charles Swithinbank on 17 January 1962 and by New Zealanders Vic McGregor, Peter Barrett, Alan Gough and Peter Le Couteur on 4 November 1963.

The cairn on Scott Nunataks December 1911. Believed to picture Hjalmar Johansen (left) and Jørgen Stubberud.—K.Prestrud

'Prestrud's Cairn' when visited on 19 December 1987.—Chris Adams

SCOTT NUNATAKS, QUEEN ALEXANDRA RANGE

Prestrud's Cairn, Scott Nunataks Queen Alexandra Range.

Norwegian Antarctic expedition

The Scott Nunataks are conspicuous twin elevations which form the northern end of the Queen Alexandra Range on Edward V11 Peninsula. They were discovered in 1902 by the Discovery expedition and named after Scott by the leader of Amundsen's eastern sledge party, Lieutenant Kristian Prestrud, who made an ascent while exploring the peninsula in 1911. "On December 2, a fairly abundant collection of specimens of all the rocks to be found there was made."

The small rock cairn at the foot of the main bluff on the north side of the nunatak was found by a New Zealand scientific party on 19 December 1987. A broken glass bottle (possibly aquavit) was nearby. The site has not been visited since.

Amundsen's station 'Framheim' has not been seen since his expedition and is presumed to have drifted out to sea in an ice berg. No structures were left by Lieutenant Nobu Shirase's expedition which called into the Bay of Whales during Amundsen's expedition.

ROCKEFELLER MOUNTAINS

Fokker Aircraft wreckage, Beryl Lake

United States Antarctic expedition

In 1987 wreckage of Richard Byrd's Fokker Super Universal high wing monoplane, "Virginia", was located by Chris Adams, Steve Weaver, Paul Broady and Peter Cleary on a frozen lake. It was wrecked in a blizzard on 13 March 1929. The Wright Whirlwind 300-hp engine and instruments were removed in December 1934 during Byrd's United States Antarctic Expedition (1933-35). The fusilage although buckled and minus its fabric is in good condition. Nearby is an American fuel and ration depot thought to have been placed in the late 1950's-early 60's.

Fokker aircraft from the United States Antarctic Expedition (1928-30), December 1987.—NZAP (Peter Cleary)

In this section, the early history and subsequent vists to historic sites in the Ross Sea region has been outlined. Already much has been done to ensure their preservation for future generations but more needs to be done. The Antarctic Heritage Trust has been established for this purpose.

Working to save the Past

Much work has taken place at the four main historic sites administered by New Zealand. In 1956-57 parties from HMNZS *Endeavour* spent considerable time clearing and cleaning the hut at Cape Royds. During the following summer the New Zealand sailors extended their efforts to include the sites at Cape Evans and Hut Point as well.

In 1960-61, New Zealand Antarctic Society volunteers led by historian Leslie Quartermain, undertook hut restoration at Cape Royds and at Cape Evans where the hut was almost completely filled with ice. At Cape Adare, during the same summer, ice was removed from Borchgrevink's living hut - the first building to be erected on the Antarctic continent - but it was not until 1963-64 that ice was removed from the Discovery expedition hut at Hut Point.

Scott Base staff and Antarctic Society 'caretakers' carried out annual maintenance at the sites until the mid-1970s. A more planned approach and greater resources however were necessary.

The Historic Sites Management Committee of the Ross Dependency Research Committee implemented a five year management plan. In 1987, Antarctic Heritage Trust was formed and has since developed a conservation and management plan now known as the Heritage Management Plan. Considerable work has been undertaken by Trust parties comprised of trained conservators, archaeologists and other specialists assisted by youth group members of the New Zealand Antarctic Programme.

The first major construction work since the 1963-64 season has focused on the attachment of new external roof fabric on the buildings at

Recladding the stables at Cape Evans in January 1989.—Neville Ritchie

Cape Evans, Cape Royds and Cape Adare. The materials used have been carefully chosen to ensure that they are aesthetically compatible with the original components, but also meet with Trust policy that all works be reversible. The Trust aims to minimise replacement, retaining the original fabric wherever possible. In tandem with this work a range of other maintenance projects has been completed.

Standard archaeological techniques, including the documentation of any stratigraphy and of all artefacts recovered in-situ, have been used in examining the stables and stores annex at Cape Evans and the stores hut at Cape Adare.

Over three decades several inventories have been taken at the major sites. In 1977-78 a list of artefacts was compiled and four years later, the first detailed photographic record was made. In 1990 the Trust, using an approved museological formula commenced a systematic computerised recording of the contents of the principal Ross Island sites with over 8000 artefacts being documented. This inventory, together with substantial photographic coverage, provides a datum for on-going conservation, security, monitoring and maintenance purposes. A container has been installed by the Trust at Scott Base to ensure the safety of artefacts awaiting conservation.

Regular monitoring of temperature, humidity and light levels, together with annual building deformation surveys of the Ross Island huts, add to the detailed conservation information being collected by the Trust for future use.

New Zealand has long recognised the need to provide direction and continuity for management of the historic sites. Objectives have been established to provide a base line for identifying planning constraints, formulating policies and for creating the best means for future action.

The Trust party at Cape Royds January 1991.Brendon Haigh, Youth Group member.—NZAP (Cath Gilmour)

Excavating the stables at Cape Evans. Roger Fyfe with percussion tool January 1992.—NZAP (Yvonne Martin)

The Heritage Management Plan is based upon internationally accepted standards such as the ICOMOS charter. It is continually updated and monitored by the Trust and provides the basis for the long-term preservation and management of the sites in the Ross Sea region, including the preparation of management plans for each historic site as provided for by the Madrid Protocol.

Major environmental problems affecting the artefacts to be found in the huts mainly relate to high relative humidity, salt damage and excessive light levels. In many cases preservation is made extremely difficult because of the range of materials involved.

Coastal sites are popular with cruise ship op-

Recording artefacts at Cape Evans January 1992. David Woodings.—NZAP (Yvonne Martin)

erators and there have been a number of other non-governmental visits in recent years. The Ross Island sites are an important recreation resource for special visitors and personnel from nearby bases. The Trust has devised a Code of Conduct for visitors and recommended guidelines for maximum numbers permitted to visit each site.

The Trust has also produced interpretive material to provide visitors with a better understanding of the necessity to protect the sites.

The scientific and inspirational rationale for maintaining the historic huts in Antarctica and conserving their contents has been succinctly portrayed by Neville Ritchie and Alexy Simmons who wrote, "It will suffice to say that the heroic era of Antarctic exploration is recognised world wide as having pre-eminent historic significance. It is characterised by well documented outstanding feats of human endurance in the face of formidable odds. The huts and associated artefacts, monuments and field depots are the tangible remains of the early expeditions. As such, they play an important role in transmitting history, traditions and values to succeeding generations. In addition, they are 'time capsules' of technological achievement and constitute an invaluable comparative data base for research, now and in the future."

The historic sites of the Ross Sea region represent significant evidence of human endeavour and are worthy of protection for future generations. Without planned professional efforts these sites will disappear. They are unique sites which derive from activities of almost a century ago. Unique sites on a unique continent, perhaps the last, loneliest and most challenging frontier of the world.

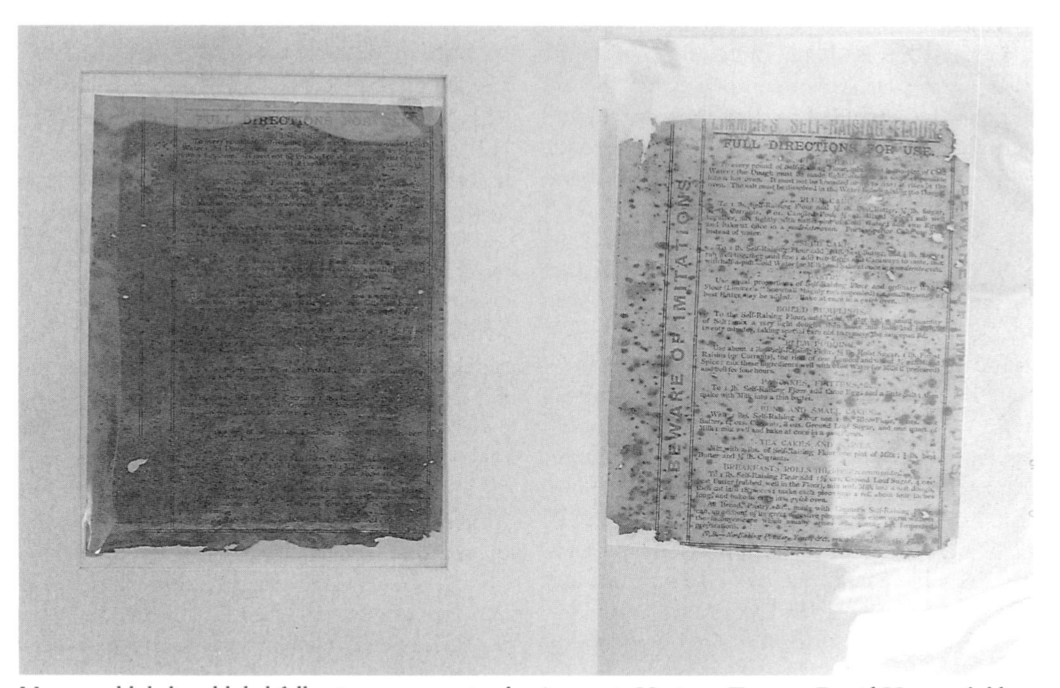

Untreated label and label following conservation by Antarctic Heritage Trust.—David Harrowfield

The Early Expeditions

1839-43 British Naval Expedition. Leader J.C.Ross. Expedition ships HMS *Erebus*, HMS *Terror* Charted 900km Victoria Land coastline. Landed on Possession Island, Franklin Island. Discovered Ross Island and Mt.Erebus, Ross Ice Shelf.

1893-95 Norwegian sealing and whaling exploration. Leader H. J. Bull. Expedition ship *Antarctic*. Landed on Svend Foyn Island, and at Cape Adare, 24 January 1895.

1898-1900 British Antarctic Expedition also termed Southern Cross expedition. Leader C.E.Borchgrevink. Expedition ship *Southern Cross*.

Landed at Cape Adare and became first party to winter on the continent. A midwinter camp, a rock shelter, built on Duke of York Island. Sledging trips in Robertson Bay. Scientific investigations included zoology, geology, meteorology, and terrestrial magnetism. Two parties sledged 16km on the Ross Ice Shelf to about 78° 50'S on 16 and 19 February 1900.

1901-04 National Antarctic Expedition also termed Discovery expedition. Leader R.F.Scott. Expedition ship *Discovery*. The relief ships *Morning* and *Terra Nova* were associated with this expedition. *Discovery* frozen in for two winters in McMurdo Sound. Building erected at Hut Point and scientific observations. The first extensive exploration on land in Antarctica; a sledge party reached 82° 16.5'S. Examined the coast of Victoria Land, the Ross Ice Shelf, discovered King Edward V11 Land and reached the South Polar Plateau. Scott Island discovered by the *Morning* on 25 December 1902.

1907-09 British Antarctic Expedition also termed Nimrod expedition. Leader E.H.Shackleton. Expedition ship *Nimrod* assisted by *Koonya*. Wintered at Cape Royds on Ross Island. First ascent of Mt.Erebus (3794m) 10 March 1908; sledged to within 01° 37' (180 km) of the South Pole, 9 January 1909; discovered nearly 800km of new mountain ranges bordering the Ross Ice Shelf; South Magnetic Pole reached 16 January 1909; first experiments with motor transport; first book, 'Aurora Australis', printed in Antarctica.

1910-12 Norwegian Antarctic Expedition. Leader R.E.G.Amundsen. Expedition ship *Fram*. Wintered on the Ross Ice Shelf at the Bay of Whales. Five men reached the South Pole, 14 December 1911. Discovered Queen Maud Mountains. Explored King Edward V11 Land.

1910-12 Japanese Antarctic Expedition. Leader N.Shirase. Expedition ship *Kainan-Maru*. In 1910-11, failed to penetrate pack ice and wintered in Sydney, Australia. During second season reached Bay of Whales, from which a party sledged some distance south-east across the Ross Ice Shelf; landed on King Edward V11 Land. Sledged 250km inland.

1910-13 British Antarctic Expedition also termed Terra Nova expedition, leader R.F.Scott. Expedition ship *Terra Nova*. Wintered at Cape Evans on Ross Island; five men reached the South Pole, 17 January 1912 by man-hauling; all died during the return journey. Extensive exploration and scientific investigations conducted (biology, geology, glaciology, meteorology, geophysics) along the coast of Victoria Land and on the Ross Ice Shelf. Midwinter sledging trip to Cape Crozier. Separate party known as the Northern Party (led by V.L.A.Campbell) wintered at Cape Adare (1911) and in an ice cave, on Inexpressible Island (1912); discovered Oates Land.

1914-17 Imperial Trans-Antarctic Expedition also termed (with respect to Ross Sea section) Ross Sea Party I.T.A.E. (Expedition ship *Aurora*) and with respect to Weddell Sea section) Weddell Sea Party I.T.A.E. (Expedition ship *Endurance*). Leader E.H.Shackleton. *Aurora* frozen in at Cape Evans for the winter. On 10 May 1915 the ship was driven from the moorings in a blizzard, leaving ten men ashore to lay depots to the Beardmore Glacier for Shackleton's proposed trans-Antarctic journey (1914-16). *Aurora* drifted for ten months in Ross Sea pack ice and got free on 14 March 1916.

1916-17 Ross Sea Relief Expedition . Leader J.K.Davis. Expedition ship, *Aurora.* Rescued seven survivors of Ross Sea Party 10 January 1917.

List of Sites

Historic sites in this section have been grouped regionally and where possible chronologically within each region. They are listed in accordance with AHT's "Heritage Management Plan" (1995).

Category 1
Sites currently listed and specifically protected by the provisions of the Antarctic Treaty.

Category 2
Sites which have been visited recently and which have importance but which do not justify specific listing in the Treaty.

Category 3
Sites with historic significance but which have little visible evidence remaining.

Most positions of latitude and longitude are taken from Geographic Names of the Antarctic (1981). These relate to the major geographic features in the vicinity rather than the exact position of the site.

The Madrid Protocol 1991 (Annex V.) recognises that Historic Sites and Monuments listed by Antarctic Treaty Consultative Meetings shall not be damaged, removed or destroyed. The list may be amended with the agreement of the Treaty Parties.

CAPE ADARE AND ROBERTSON BAY

1. Huts on Ridley Beach, Cape Adare. (Lat 71° 18' S, Long 170° 09' E.)
Living hut and stores hut erected February 1899 by the Southern Cross expedition. Also the remains of hut from the Northern Party, 1911-12. Only Borchgrevink's living hut survives in a reasonable state of repair.
(Antarctic Treaty list No.22, Category 1)

2. Hanson's grave at Cape Adare. (Lat 71° 17'S., Long 170° 15' E. - position from Treaty list)
Nicolai Hanson, a Norwegian biologist was a member of the Southern Cross expedition, who died 14 October 1899. This is the first known grave in the Antarctic. (Antarctic Treaty list No.23, Category 1)

3. Supply depot, Ridley Beach, Cape Adare. Placed in 1899 by the Southern Cross expedition. (Category 2)

4. Supply depot, Cape Adare. Presumed placed on top of Adare Peninsula above Ridley Beach in 1899 by the Southern Cross expedition. Remnant believed seen 1990. (Category 3)

5. Supply depot with cairn and camp site, Cape Adare. Placed in 1912 by the Northern Party of the Terra Nova expedition 1910-13. Inspected in1990. (Category 2)

6. Camp site, east shore Robertson Bay, Cape Adare. Placed in 1899 by the Southern Cross expedition. Not seen since 1899. (Category 3)

7. Rock hut, Duke of York Island, Robertson Bay. (Lat 71° 38' S, 170° 04' E). Erected as a winter camp by the Southern Cross expedition in 1899. Area inspected 1982 but site not seen. (Category 2)

8. Supply depot, Crescent Bay, Duke of York Island. (Lat 71° 37' S, Long 170° 04' E.). Placed in 1899 by the Southern Cross expedi-

tion. No known sighting since 1899. (Category 3)

9. Cave, Penelope Point, Robertson Bay. (Lat 71° 30' S, Long 169° 36'E). Used by the Northern Party in 1911. Site viewed from helicopter 1990 but no ground inspection. (Category 2)

POSSESSION ISLANDS

10. Message post Svend Foyn Island, Possession Islands. (Lat 71° 56' S, Long 171° 04' E.) Placed in 1895 by the ship *Antarctic* . Seen early 1965. (Antarctic Treaty Consultative Meeting XIX, 1995, Category 1)

COULMAN ISLAND

11. Message post, Cape Wadworth, Coulman Island. (Lat 73° 19' S. Long 169° 47' E.)
Placed 1902 by Discovery expedition. Seen 1989 - 90. (Antarctic Treaty Consultative Meeting XIX, 1995, Category 1)

TERRA NOVA BAY

12. Site of ice cave, Inexpressible Island. (Lat 74° 53' S, Long 163° 44' E.) Constructed in March 1912 by the Northern Party. The party spent the winter of 1912 in this shelter. (Antarctic Treaty list No.14, Category 1)

13. Supply depot, Hells Gate Moraine, Inexpressible Island. (Lat 74° 53' S, Long 163° 44' E.) Placed on 25 January 1913 at close of Terra Nova expedition . Contents removed by AHT for conservation in January 1995. (Antarctic Treaty Consultative Meeting XIX, 1995, Category 1)

HUT POINT, ROSS ISLAND

14. Building at Hut Point, Ross Island. (Lat 77° 51' S, Long 166° 38'E.) Erected in February 1902 by the Discovery expedition. (Antarctic Treaty list No.18, Category 1)

15. Cross at Hut Point, Ross Island. Erected in February 1904 by the Discovery expedition, in memory of G.T.Vince, a member of that expedition who died in the vicinity in 1902. (Antarctic Treaty list No.19, Category 1)

CAPE ROYDS, ROSS ISLAND

16. Building at Cape Royds, Ross Island. (Lat 77° 33' S, Long 166° 07' E.) Erected in February 1908 by the Nimrod expedition. There are various depots in the vicinity. (Antarctic Treaty list No.15, Category 1)

CAPE EVANS, ROSS ISLAND

17. Building at Cape Evans, Ross Island. (Lat 77° 38' S, Long 166° 25' E.) Erected in January 1911 by the Terra Nova expedition, and the main base of the Ross Sea Party. (Antarctic Treaty list No.16, Category 1)

18. Cross on Wind Vane Hill. (Lat 77° 38'S, Long 166° 24'E.) Erected by the Ross Sea Party in memory of Mackintosh, Hayward and Rev. Spencer-Smith who died in the vicinity in 1916. (Antarctic Treaty list No.17, Category 1)

CAPE CROZIER, ROSS ISLAND

19. Message post, Cape Crozier, Ross Island. (Lat 77° 27'S, Long 169° 16'E.) Erected in 1902

by Discovery expedition. (Antarctic Treaty Consultative Meeting XIX, 1995, Category 1)

20. Rock hut Cape Crozier, Ross Island. (Lat 77° 31' S, Long 169° 24' E.) Constructed in July 1911 by Edward Wilson's party (Terra Nova expedition) during the winter journey to collect emperor penguin eggs. (Antarctic Treaty list No.21, Category 1)

MT CIS, ROSS ISLAND

21. Supply depot, Mount Cis,near Cape Barne, Ross Island. (Lat 77° 35' S, Long 166° 13' E.) Presumed placed in 1912 during the Terra Nova expedition. Inspected 1977. (Category 2)

OBSERVATION HILL, ROSS ISLAND

22. Cross on Observation Hill, Ross Island. (Lat 77° 51' S, Long 166° 40' E.) Erected in January 1913 by the Terra Nova expedition, in memory of Scott, Bowers, Wilson, Oates, Evans who perished on the return journey from the South Pole March 1912. (Antarctic Treaty list No.20, Category 1)

FERRAR GLACIER, SOUTH VICTORIA LAND

23. Supply depot, Ferrar Glacier. (Lat 77° 46' S, Long 163° 00' E.) Placed 1902 by Discovery expedition. Located 1957 but not seen in recent years. (Category 3)

24. Supply depot, Cathedral Rocks. (Lat 77° 51' S, Long 162° 30'E.) Placed by Griffith Taylor's geological party during the Terra Nova expedition. Last known sighting 1911. (Category 3)

DAVIS BAY, (now Salmon Bay), SOUTH VICTORIA LAND

25. Supply depot, Davis Bay, McMurdo Sound. (Lat 77° 56' S, Long164° 33' E. - from Helm 1958) Placed by Griffith Taylor's geological party during the Terra Nova expedition. Last known sighting 1911. (Category 3)

GRANITE HARBOUR, SOUTH VICTORIA LAND

26. Rock Hut, "Granite House" Cape Geology. (Lat 77° 00'S, Long 162° 32' E.) Built during the Terra Nova expedition by Griffith Taylor's second western geological party. (Antarctic Treaty Consultative Meeting XIX, 1995, Category 1)

27. Camp site Devils Punchbowl, Granite Harbour. (Lat 77° 01'S, Long 162° 24'E.) Placed by Griffith Taylor's geological party during the Terra Nova expedition. Last known sighting 1911. (Category 3)

CAPE ROBERTS, SOUTH VICTORIA LAND

28. Supply depot and cairn Cape Roberts. (Lat 77° 02' S. Long 163° 12' E.) Placed in 1912 by Griffith Taylor's geological party during the Terra Nova expedition. Located 1957. Not seen in recent years. (Category 3)

DEPOT ISLAND, ROSS SEA

29. Supply depot, Depot Island. (Lat 76° 42' S, Long 162° 58' E.) Presumed to have been placed in 1908 during the Nimrod expedition. Last visited 1984. (Category 3)

CAPE BERNACCHI, SOUTH VICTORIA LAND

30. Campsite, supply depot and cairn, Cape Bernacchi. (Lat 77° 29' S, Long 163° 51' E.) Placed by Griffith Taylor's geological party during the Terra Nova expedition. Last known sighting 1912. (Category 3)

BUTTER POINT, SOUTH VICTORIA LAND

31. Supply depot, Butter Point, Bowers Piedmont Glacier. (Lat 77° 39' S, Long 164° 14' E.) Associated with the Terra Nova expedition . Remaining contents recovered 1988, nothing now known to exist. (Category 3)

QUEEN MAUD MOUNTAINS

32. Rock cairn, Mount Betty, Queen Maud Mountains. (Lat 85° 11' S, Long 163° 45' W.) Known as 'Amundsen's Cairn'. Erected by Roald Amundsen on 6 January 1912, on his return from the South Pole to 'Framheim'. (Antarctic Treaty list No.24, Category 1)

QUEEN ALEXANDRA RANGE

33. Rock cairn, Scott Nunataks, Queen Alexandra Range. (Lat 77° 12.3' S, Long 154° 30' W.) Laid 2 December 1911 and known as Prestrud's Cairn after the leader of Amundsen's eastern sledge party. Inspected 1987-88. (Antarctic Treaty Consultative Meeting XIX, 1995, Category 1)

ROCKEFELLER MOUNTAINS

34. Fokker aircraft wreckage, Beryl Lake near Washington Ridge, Rockefeller Mountains. (Lat 78° 06' S, Long 154° 48' W.). Richard Byrd's aircraft wrecked at field camp in a blizzard 1929. Inspected 24 December 1987. (Category 2)

Selected Bibliography

Alberts, G. Ed. Geographic Names of the Antarctic.
United States Board of Geographic Names. (1981)

Antarctic Heritage Trust . Heritage Mangement Plan
Christchurch.(1987)

Antarctic Heritage Trust. Historic Sites. Ross Sea Region Antarctica.
Conservation Plan. C.Cochran Ed. Antarctic Heritage Trust, Christchurch. (1990)

Bernacchi, L. To The South Polar Regions
Hurst and Blackett, London. (1901)

Cherry-Garrard, A. The Worst Journey In The World
Constable & Company, London.(1922)

Harrowfield, D.L. Sledging Into History
Macmillan, Auckland. (1981)

Headland, R.K. Chronological List of Antarctic Expeditions and Related Historical Events.
Cambridge University Press, Cambridge. (1989)

Heap, John Ed. Handbook of the Antarctic Treaty System Pt.3
Polar Publications SPRI Cambridge. (1990)

Helm, A.S. Provisional Gazatteer of the Ross Dependency
Government Printer, Wellington. (1958)

Hillary, E. No Latitude for Error
Hodder & Stoughton, London.(1961)

Mackintosh, A.L.A. Shackleton's Lieutenant . The Nimrod diary of A. L. A Mackintosh, British Antarctic Expedition 1907-09
Edited by S.F.Newman, Polar Publications Auckland. (1990)

Priestley, R.E. Antarctic Adventure-Scott's Northern Party
T.Fisher Unwin, London (1914)

Readers Digest, Antarctica- Great Stories From The Frozen Continent
Readers Digest Services Pty Ltd, Sydney. (1985)

Richards, R.W. The Ross Sea Party 1914-17
Scott Polar Research Institute, Cambridge.(1962)

Ross, M.J. Ross In The Antarctic
Caedmon of Whitby, England. (1982)

Quartermain, L.B. Two Huts in the Antarctic
Government Printer, Wellington.(1963)

Quartermain, L.B. South To The Pole
Oxford University Press, London.(1977)

Scientific Committee on Antarctic Research. The Protocol on Environmental Protection To The Antarctic Treaty, With Annexes, Done At Madrid 4 October 1991.
Scientific Committee On Antarctic Research, Cambridge.(1992)

Turner, G.A. A Strategy for the Preservation and Management of Historic Sites in Ross Dependency Antarctica.
Department of Lands and Survey, Wellington. (1979)

Turner, G.A. and Harrowfield, D.L. Corporate Strategic Plan for Ross Island Historic Sites, Ross Dependency Antarctica
Ross Dependency Research Committee. (1984)

Glossary

AHT - Antarctic Heritage Trust

BANZARE - British Australian New Zealand Antarctic Research Expedition (1929-31)

CAG - Conservation Advisory group

CIROS - Cenozoic Investigation in the Ross Sea

DOSLI - Department of Survey and Land Information

DSIR - Department of Scientific and Industrial Research

FRS - Fellow of the Royal Society

GANOVEX - German Antarctic North Victoria Land Expedition

HMNZS - Her Majesty's New Zealand Ship

HSMC - Historic Sites Management Committee

ICAIR - International Centre for Antarctic Information and Research

ICOMOS - International Charter for the Conservation and Restoration of Monuments and Sites.

IGY - International Geophysical Year (1957-58)

NSF - National Science Foundation

NZAP - New Zealand Antarctic Programme

NZARP - New Zealand Antarctic Research Programme

RDRC - Ross Dependency Research Committee

RIM - Royal Indian Marine

RN - Royal Navy

RNR - Royal Naval Reserve

RNZAF - Royal New Zealand Air Force

RNZN - Royal New Zealand Navy

TAE - Commonwealth Trans Antarctic Expedition (1955-58)

Index